# D.I.Y.

## Internet Marketing
## for Beginners

Library of Congress Control Number: 2014904780

ISBN: 978-0-9960055-0-0

1. Reference / General

2. Business / Internet Marketing

This book is published in the United States of America

# D.I.Y.

## Internet Marketing
## for Beginners

A *Playbook* for Increasing Your Online Presence

Angela Schnaubelt

(Coach Angela)

## IN DEDICATION

*To my Father, James F. Schnaubelt, who instilled the work ethic in me, taught me how to critically think and read, and who was my hero in so many ways. Thanks, Dad.*

# TABLE OF CONTENTS

Acknowledgments . . . . . . . . . . . . . . . . . . . . . . . . . . . . 13

Foreword . . . . . . . . . . . . . . . . . . . . . . . . . . . . . . . . 15

**SECTION I: BASICS** . . . . . . . . . . . . . . . . . . . . . . . . . **17**

Chapter 1: Introduction . . . . . . . . . . . . . . . . . . . . . . 19

Overwhelming Catchwords and Phrases

The Big "Why" is the Sense of Community

The Difference Between Traditional Marketing and Internet Marketing

Social Media is Social

Have Fun Expanding Your Online Presence

Understanding the Big Picture

Reasonable Expectations and R.O.I.

Are You Ready? Getting Started!

Chapter 2: A Few Quick Case Studies . . . . . . . . . . . . . . . . 31

Andrea

Robert

And the Big Story

Chapter 3: The Benefits of Online Marketing and Social Media . . . . . . . . . . .35

Benefits of Online Marketing

Build Brand Awareness

Keep an Eye on Your Competitors

Spread the Word About Promotions/Deals/Sales

Increase Customer Loyalty

Increase Participants in Social or Charitable Causes

Viral Effect

Higher Quality of Dialog

Ability to Refine Advertisements and Your Message

Reach Tightly-Defined Demographics

Manage Your Reputation

How to Maximize the Benefits

Improve Search Engine Rankings Through Keywords

Develop Backlinks to Your Website From Other Websites

Establish Yourself as an Expert

Try to go Viral

Chapter 4: Foundations . . . . . . . . . . . . . . . . . . . . . . .47

Introduction

The Demographics of Your Customers

Mission Statement

Listening and Humility

**SECTION II: PLATFORMS, TOOLS AND TACTICS.** . . . . . . . . . . . . . . . **63**

Introduction

What is the Difference Between Platforms, Tools and Tactics?

Chapter 5: Platforms . . . . . . . . . . . . . . . . . . . . . . . . 67

Website . . . . . . . . . . . . . . . . . . . . . . . . . . .69

Website Architecture

Mobile Websites

Content: Articles and Videos

Facebook . . . . . . . . . . . . . . . . . . . . . . . . . .79

Facebook Fans

Posting on Facebook

Facebook Ads

Facebook Applications

YouTube . . . . . . . . . . . . . . . . . . . . . . . . . . 89

Setting Up a YouTube Channel

Types of Videos and Video Campaigns

Video Production Quality

Twitter . . . . . . . . . . . . . . . . . . . . . . . . . . . 95

Setting Up Your Twitter Account

Twitter and Your Branding

Increasing Your Exposure on Twitter

What to Tweet

LinkedIn . . . . . . . . . . . . . . . . . . . . . . . . . . 105

Setting Up Your LinkedIn Account

Google+ . . . . . . . . . . . . . . . . . . . . . . . . . . 111

Google+ Circles

Google+ Hangouts

Google+ Events

Google Communities

Setting Up Your Google+ Account

Daily Deals and Check-in Sites . . . . . . . . . . . . . . . . . . 117

Blogs and Vlogs . . . . . . . . . . . . . . . . . . . . . . . 121

Frequency of Posting Blog Articles and Vlog Videos

Length of Articles and Videos

Types of Articles and Videos

Leveraging Your Blog Article or Vlog Video

Event Promotions and Meetup Sites . . . . . . . . . . . . . . . . 129

Meetup.com

Plancast.com

Eventbrite.com

Advertising an Offer

Online Directories and Reviews . . . . . . . . . . . . . . . . . . . . . . . . . 141
    Online Directories
    Customer Review Websites
Chapter 6: Tools and Tactics. . . . . . . . . . . . . . . . . . . . . . . . . .153
    What are Tools and Tactics?
    List of Tools . . . . . . . . . . . . . . . . . . . . . . . . . . . . . . . . . . . . 157
        Automatic Tools for Posting Content
        Facebook Applications
        Analytics
        Affiliate Programs
        Webinars, Classes, eBooks, and DVDs
        Sophisticated Opt-Ins and Ad Copy
    List of Tactics . . . . . . . . . . . . . . . . . . . . . . . . . . . . . . . . . . 163
        Search Engine Optimization (SEO)
        Webinar Swaps
        Social Bookmarking
        Pinterest
        Email Campaigns
        Ad Campaigns
        PPC/Google Adword Campaigns
        Facebook Ad Campaigns
        Content Leveraging
        Professional Branding
        Phone Applications
        Blog Monetization
        Offering a DVD or eBook

**SECTION III: STRATEGY AND CONTENT** . . . . . . . . . . . . . . . . . . . . . . .173
    Chapter 7: Strategy . . . . . . . . . . . . . . . . . . . . . . . . . . . . . . . . 175
        Introduction
        Your Online Marketing Plan
    Chapter 8: Content . . . . . . . . . . . . . . . . . . . . . . . . . . . . . . . . 181
        Introduction
        Content: Text
        Article Ideas
        Length of Articles
        Article Webs
        Content: Videos
        Content: Pictures
        Content: Comments
        Content: Tweets

Content: Facebook
Creating an Editorial Calendar for Your Content

**SECTION IV: CONCLUSION** . . . . . . . . . . . . . . . . . . . . . . . . . . . . . . **195**
   Chapter 9: Conclusion . . . . . . . . . . . . . . . . . . . . . . . . .197
      Putting it All Together . . . . . . . . . . . . . . . . . . . 199
      Steps to Implement for Internet Marketing . . . . . . . . . . . . . 199
         Listen
         Branding/niche
         Mission Statement
         Platforms & Strategy
         Create content
         Implementation & Tactics
         Analyze & Tweak Strategy
         Repeat steps 1 through 7

**APPENDICES** . . . . . . . . . . . . . . . . . . . . . . . . . . . . . . . . . . . . **203**
   Appendix A
      Online Presence Assessment . . . . . . . . . . . . . . . . .203
      Online Marketing Plan Template . . . . . . . . . . . . . . . . 209
   Appendix B
      Master Password List . . . . . . . . . . . . . . . . . . . . 213
   Appendix C
      Tracking Sheets for Platform Activity . . . . . . . . . . . . . .217
         Facebook fans
         Facebook posts
         YouTube
         Twitter
         LinkedIn
         Event promotion
   Appendix D
      Resources . . . . . . . . . . . . . . . . . . . . . . . 225
   Appendix E
      Glossary . . . . . . . . . . . . . . . . . . . . . . . . 227
   Appendix F
      Coach Angela's Mantras . . . . . . . . . . . . . . . . . . 237

# ACKNOWLEDGMENTS

I could not have written this book without the love, prayers, encouragement, and literal support of my best friend, Robert Bowen. Thanks specifically to my family: my brilliant and supportive sister, Teri Schnaubelt, and her husband, Tim Pritts; as well as my loving cousins, Jeff and Annie Schnaubelt.

Thanks to all of you who supported and helped me with financial aid, love, encouragement and prayers during my battle with stage IV cervical and rectal cancer. I got through it thanks to all of you, and I was able to finish my book.

Special thanks to Chance McLin, who sponsored this book in the publishing process, and for his belief in me that I was worthy of publishing. Thanks to Donna Whitaker, who donated her professional editing expertise in the final phase. Also, thanks to George Edgar for his encouragement and support to write the first draft, and to Josh Whitaker's creative support to publish the first, local run.

Finally, thanks to Joyce Feustel, a baby boomer social media tutor, who gave constructive advice towards the final draft.

# FOREWORD

Angela Schnaubelt (aka Coach Angela) has produced a much-needed social media user's guide and resource in this book *D.I.Y. Internet Marketing for Beginners: A Playbook for Increasing Your Online Presence.* Her book is very accessible, practical and hands-on rather than filled with complex marketing terms and strategies.

Many of the books on social media marketing are written for the relatively experienced and social savvy marketer. There are very few that are directed to the social media novice and intermediate level user of social media.

As a social media tutor and training, frequently working with small business owners, I know the importance of developing written materials on social media that are easy for the social media newcomer to follow and understand. These people will definitely benefit from access to this very comprehensive book as a go-to resource.

Coach Angela takes the mystery out of social media marketing with her refreshing "back to the basics" approach in both the format and language of this book. This is just the kind of book that business owners should have at their fingertips when they are embarking on their social media marketing journey. And then they should revisit this book when they are tweaking their social media marketing efforts.

There are so many aspects of this book that I find appealing. For example, I like the way the book is organized by addressing the benefits of online marketing and social media; providing specifics about the most commonly used social media platforms, tools and tactics; offering specific ideas related to the content of social media activity; and then pulling everything together in the last section with steps for the reader to implement.

I also appreciate how Coach Angela has a section for people who are just beginning their social media marketing followed by a section for the more intermediate user. She does a great job of encouraging the reader to stretch beyond their comfort level and try some new strategies.

Other attractive aspects of the book are the tools she provides in the way of worksheets, tear-out sheets, glossary and other very practical tools. Using this approach should make it more likely for the person reading this book to roll up their sleeves and actually employ the exercises that she recommends.

It is an honor and delight to write this foreword for Coach Angela. Hats off to her for creating a much-needed book that can be readily used by anyone wanting to improve their social media marketing efforts and get the results they want.

Joyce Feustel
Founder, Boomers' Social Media Tutor

# SECTION I
## BASICS

# NOTES

# CHAPTER 1
# INTRODUCTION

Congratulations on making the decision to take a closer look at the game of online marketing and social media! If you are totally mystified by it, don't feel alone. Many people are—even some who claim they aren't. This Playbook will walk you through step by step to explain how the whole thing works, give you a glossary so you can understand the lingo, and equip you with practical easy-to-understand strategies to facilitate your success.

Social media is only one component of Internet marketing. This Playbook will demystify the language and concepts of Internet marketing for beginners and help intermediate players to step up their game.

This isn't about whether you use social media or not. Your customers use it. Your customers are online every single day. They use their mobile phones to access the Internet, even if *you* are not.

Your customers are using Foursquare and Yelp and Google Places. They are researching before they shop, looking up reviews. They are checking out your business online whether you know it or not. They are watching YouTube videos for entertainment and also for how-to information – even if *you* are not.

This isn't about you. It's about them.

Prospects can come to you from stumbling on your business online, but you do not know where or when this might happen. Increasing your online presence will help you reach prospects, gain their trust, and put you in control of your marketing.

Yes, there is more to the online marketing world than just having a website and a Facebook page. Use this Playbook to get your arms around all the platforms the Internet has to offer so you can use them effectively for marketing.

# NOTES

What should you focus on? There is so much to do! And no shortage of advice coming from colleagues and social media experts of what has worked for them or of what they heard that one should do. Should you have a Facebook page? If so, what should you be doing with it? Should you make some videos? If so, what sort of videos? What type of articles should you be posting on your website or blog?

This Playbook will help you create a strategy so that you can proceed and implement with more purpose, less confusion, and more excitement!

## OVERWHELMING CATCHWORDS AND PHRASES

Check the glossary in the back of the book if you don't understand a word or phrase. This book will make even the earliest beginner less intimidated.

Don't worry about all the chatter, buzzwords, and acronyms. We will keep the fancy terms to a minimum. After working your way through this Playbook, you will have a solid foundation of all the terms currently used for social media. You'll get the hang of it!

Some of the catch phrases come with myths, so keep an open mind when you read through this Playbook. Just because everybody tells you that you should do something does not necessarily mean that you should do it. Stay in your truth, and only do what resonates with you. We will talk about business values and your mission statement in Chapter 4.

## THE BIG "WHY" IS THE SENSE OF COMMUNITY

You do not have a strong enough "why" for using the Internet for marketing, or you would already be rockin' and rollin' with your activities online, and you wouldn't be reading this book right now.

Remember, it's not about you. It's about them.

So, what's the big appeal? Why is the Internet so popular? Even if you don't use it for anything more than a huge, immediate encyclopedic source of information, others use it for social reasons.

Your big "why" is the sense of community. Humans are social animals. Yes, we need each other for physical survival, but we also rely on each other for emotional support. Our identity is tied in with whom we associate, with whom we depend, and with whom we interact.

Decades ago, the community was more literal. Those who lived in a close geographic area were considered a community: people lived, worked, worshiped and played together.

If half the hardware store in town was wiped out in a tornado, the entire community would help to rebuild it. Even if you didn't like the owner, you would help. Why? Because you needed him and his store. Because it was expected of you. Because everyone stuck together.

# NOTES

What changed? Technology. Technological advances affected our sense of community. When cars were invented, you could just drive to the next town and not buy from the local hardware store owner. You didn't need him as much. Fast forward to airplanes and the Internet and you can buy from a hardware store in Australia or directly from a hardware manufacturer in China.

But we humans are social creatures. To compensate for the disintegration of the local communities, we use the Internet to drill down our niche interests and congregate with others just like us. We can play and interact with others online, but others of our choosing – others just like us.

Your big "why" for participating in Internet marketing as a business is the sense of community. It's about your prospects, not about you and your business. It's about their very real sense of community.

Consider this: how many women friends could a single mom who is a lesbian, a Rottweiler breeder, a pink depression-era glass collector, and a Harley riding sober pagan find in a rural town in America? Not many. How many friends could she find online who would accept her interests and her identity just as she is? Even if she never meets them in person, her small online community of like-minded women are real to her. It's important to her, it's real to her.

Even if you can't relate to the example of the rural lesbian above, you need to understand the importance of the sense of community to people using the Internet. When you participate online as a business, the rules of community apply. You need to respect the community as its own unit and interact accordingly.

The sense of community is the big "why." Use this as your anchor, as your reason, for playing the game of Internet marketing. Go to the prospects and customers where they are. And when they get to know you, like you and trust you, then they will do business with you or refer business to you.

## THE DIFFERENCE BETWEEN TRADITIONAL MARKETING AND INTERNET MARKETING

A successful marketing program should include elements of both traditional and online activities. This book is not about picking one form of marketing over the other. Rather, it is to let you evaluate the advantages of both so you can decide how much of each—traditional or online marketing – is right for you. It will give you tools to make a rational decision how to allocate your resources and leverage all your marketing efforts.

There are two main differences. Firstly, Internet marketing is pull marketing (in-bound marketing), where the prospects come to you when they are ready versus traditional push marketing where you are simply pushing out a static message through mainstream media. Secondly, while

# NOTES

not completely free, Internet marketing is vastly cheaper than traditional marketing.

Make no mistake. There are no shortcuts to marketing. Word of mouth from happy customers is still every bit as valuable as it ever was. Customer service and customer retention are every bit as important as they ever were in terms of being an important part of your marketing strategy. A bird in hand is worth two in the bush! Hang on to your current customers and treat them like gold. You can serve them online, as well.

Online marketing consists of more than just your website, an online shopping cart, and the social media sites such as Facebook, Twitter, and LinkedIn.

Online, or "in-bound" marketing has more potential than traditional marketing due to the elimination of mass marketing and the allowance for hyper-niche marketing. Also, it allows the customers to come to you on their own terms, interact with your company or brand, and express and solidify their loyalty. Online marketing is not static – it's dynamic.

Remember the dynamics. It's not only about the production and posting of advertisements online; it's a dynamic form of communication. The dynamics of Internet marketing allows you to communicate with niche demographics that can enhance customer service, increase customer loyalty, and so much more. Adhere to the etiquette of online communities, and you will safely navigate these dynamics.

## SOCIAL MEDIA IS SOCIAL

Social media marketing is online marketing but with an interactive twist. With social media, you can dialogue with your audience, tailor the message to certain groups, and get instant feedback that allows you to alter your message, your audience, or maybe even what you are selling.

After all social media is, well, "social." And business is not social, it's business, right? We've all been indoctrinated with the message: "never mix business with pleasure." Yet, we also hear that business (sales, specifically – which drives business) is about relationship-building. So, is it business or social?

It's both! The key is to use social media and technology as a tool and not to let the tool dominate or overwhelm you. The key, more importantly, is to wield the tool wisely so as to get maximum return and the most efficient use out of it. You need to leverage the technology (social media and the Internet) in socially-appropriate ways that will benefit your business: brand awareness, reputation management, promotions, trust-building, customer service, etc.

So, use social media as a tool to build relationships, just as you would use a happy hour business networking event, for example, as a tool to prospect and to build relationships.

# NOTES

## HAVE FUN EXPANDING YOUR ONLINE PRESENCE

This book is a Playbook, not a workbook, because it is meant to encourage you to have fun while expanding your online presence. Yes, it's business. However, since some of the online tactics and activities are time consuming, you must be engaged and excited about social media in order to be successful. It has to be fun or you will de-prioritize it, justify the de-prioritization, and then abandon it altogether. It has to be fun and it has to be personal to your business.

Use this Playbook as a planning tool, a tracking tool, a notebook for creative engagement ideas (e.g. polls, fan contests), and a guide to help you understand how all of the platforms are tied together for effective leverage of content.

Once established in the online world of social media, you can then decide what you want to maintain and what you want to outsource to professionals. You cannot get to the stage of deciding what to outsource, though, until you understand the big picture, your strategy, and your budget. You can implement what is fun for you and outsource what is difficult or time consuming, yet important.

## UNDERSTANDING THE BIG PICTURE

Before you come up with a strategy and clarify your purpose, it's mandatory to understand the big picture. You can't drill down the specifics of your strategy for online marketing unless you have a firm handle on the big picture.

Get a firm grasp of this whole Internet marketing thing, and you won't become distracted down the road. Armed with a good knowledge of the big picture, you will be able to stay in your truth, stay the course (or correct the course, if needed), and justify your decisions.

This Playbook starts with the platforms. A platform is a stage upon which you stand to deliver your message. A platform facilitates interactions online. Interactions and messages could be simple 140-character messages called tweets; videos; articles; even curated or reposted content. Once you understand the business applications of the online platforms, you can then choose just two or three upon which to focus your energy and resources.

This Playbook then touches briefly on tools and tactics so that you have a primer of the concepts to create an initial Online Marketing Plan. Delving deeper into tools and tactics will come later for you, as your sophistication increases and you are ready to outsource to Internet marketing professionals.

Now that you understand the big "why" (humans are social animals and congregate online in communities that are very real to them), you can move through the book to learn about the pieces of the big picture. Only then can you come up with a formal strategy for online marketing. One step at a time.

# NOTES

## REASONABLE EXPECTATIONS AND R.O.I.

Take the long view with Internet marketing. Reasonable expectations will help you keep your sanity when navigating the stormy seas of the vast Internet. You are not going to spruce up your website and create a Facebook page and expect that suddenly the customers will come pouring in to your store.

Reasonable expectations include understanding the synergistic effect of all your activities online and knowing that factors come into play such as credibility, trust, brand, and reputation – factors that you can't attach a number to in terms of ROI.

Expectations should be in alignment with the end goal. For example, if your end goal is evaluating your reputation so that you can initiate a reputation management campaign, then you should not expect that the listening activities (you are "listening" to online conversations about your company to gauge your online reputation) should bring in new customers.

If you are wondering what the R.O.I. will be on your Internet marketing investments, you are asking the wrong question. Many in the industry redefine R.O.I. to mean return on interaction. It's a complex strategy that includes conversations with customers and prospects that may or may not directly lead to increased business.

Don't obsess over the R.O.I., have reasonable expectations, and have lots of patience when it comes to looking at results. Take the long view.

This is the initial attitude we should take as we embark on Internet marketing as total beginners. As your sophistication grows, you can delve more deeply into analytics and the "science" of your marketing activities in terms of measurement and return.

## ARE YOU READY? GETTING STARTED!

If you are ready to jump in, let's get started. This Online Marketing Playbook will help you with the following:

1. Gain an understanding of the game of online marketing – the "why" in addition to the "how."
2. Teach you the basics of how to begin your increasing online presence.
3. Create a strategic game plan for increasing your online presence and increase its reach.
4. Track your progress with increasing your reach and posting good content.
5. Keep all your login information and passwords in one place!
6. Serve as a reference you keep returning to, as your sophistication increases over time.

Remember, this book is geared for the extreme beginner. Take courage!

# NOTES

# CHAPTER 2
# A FEW QUICK CASE STUDIES

Here are three short case studies on how Internet marketing tangibly increases business and wins elections.

## ANDREA'S STORY

"Wow, the number of students in my QiGong classes has tripled in just a few months of using Meetup.com! I never knew what a hidden treasure that website could be for business," said Andrea Sullivan, a 5-Element QiGong teacher in Minneapolis, MN. She wanted to participate in online marketing to get the word out about her classes. Frustrated with how static her website was, and lacking a calendar of events, she wanted to expand her online reach but remain hyper-local.

Andrea smiles, now, when you ask her about marketing. "The collaboration opportunities are amazing. I'm having so much fun." Andrea not only started her own group on Meetup.com (Twin Cities Tai Chi and QiGong), but she offers to teach classes for other Meetup.com groups such as Geek Physique and Body, Mind, Circle yoga, as well.

Andrea's class has become so successful that she decided to run a second class—one that fills up quickly on a weekly basis.

## ROBERT'S STORY

"I was really getting discouraged that readership in my online news column was so static," said Robert Bowen, a citizen journalist. "After a month of following the strategy Coach Angela taught me, my readership went up 800%. It took work, but the work paid off."

Robert was aware of social media, but did not really know how to use it to reach more people. Like so many of the pre-computer generation, Robert didn't understand simple things many

# NOTES

online geeks take for granted. He learned how to use Facebook, Twitter, LinkedIn, and social bookmarking sites like StumbleUpon to extend his reach. He learned the use of key works to make his articles more visible on search engines.

## AND THE BIG STORY

The presidential campaign in 2012 cost over $2 billion dollars. Most of that money was spent on advertising: TV ads, radio ads, newspaper ads, flyers, posters and the like. Some of the money was spent on social media and social media advertising. One candidate focused more on traditional advertising; the other balanced his with social media. The candidate who won was the social media savvy candidate.

Whether you voted for him or the other guy, or didn't vote at all, political experts all agree that President Obama's extensive use of social media was the difference – at least from an organizational sense – in the campaign's success. Political operatives are all studying how the Obama campaign used social media so effectively.

Social media will be a huge part of every political campaign moving into the future, as the "digital natives" (a word coined by Marc Prensky, author and video game developer that refers to the generation that was born with and grew up with the Internet and technology) come of age and start running the campaigns.

The Obama campaign used social media to communicate with the public. They used it to get their targeted messages out to specific groups like women, young people, minorities, seniors, middle class voters. They could target their message to each demographic. We are going to tightly define your business' demographics in Chapter 4 of this Playbook.

They also used social media to announce campaign events. They used it to sign up volunteers, and get volunteers to specific places on specific dates when and where they were needed.

The Obama campaign used social media to get out the vote. They tracked in real time whether their supporters had voted, and used Twitter and Facebook to get them to the polls. Twitter was instrumental in keeping voters to stay put in long lines at the polls, and dispelled lies initially spread meant to disenfranchise voters.

Using the Internet, a volunteer could agree to make one call or a dozen depending on their time. They could do it from home or anywhere because all they had to do was log in, get a name and phone number, and make the call.

In the end, this social media and Internet effort forever changed the way campaigns will be conducted. Once you understand the true power and potential of the Internet, you, too, will be forever changed in the way you look at and plan your marketing and advertising activities.

# NOTES

# CHAPTER 3
# THE BENEFITS OF ONLINE MARKETING AND SOCIAL MEDIA

What are the specific benefits of online marketing? Your investments of time and money can't always be measured in terms of monetary ROI (return on investment), so you need to understand there are both tangible and intangible benefits of social media and online marketing.

# NOTES

# BENEFITS OF ONLINE MARKETING

Here are some of the benefits of online marketing and how it compares to traditional marketing. Remember, you can always refer to the glossary in the back of this book if you run across terms that are unfamiliar to you.

## BUILD BRAND AWARENESS

Traditional advertising increases exposure. You participate in online marketing for the same reason—to increase exposure. Your online presence helps to raise brand awareness, solidify recognition, and build trust among customers and prospects alike.

## KEEP AN EYE ON YOUR COMPETITORS

Internet marketing allows you to keep an eye on the competition. Keep your friends close and your enemies closer. Keep close tabs on what the competition is doing in terms of their marketing positioning and their online reputation.

Look for creative alliance opportunities to turn those perceived enemies into collaborative partners. Model yourself after successful competitors' activities: are they offering sophisticated opt-ins or do they have a lot of fans on their Facebook page? How often are they tweeting?

## SPREAD THE WORD ABOUT PROMOTIONS/DEALS/SALES

You can use the Internet and social media to offer promotions to attract new customers. Online methods of announcing deal promotions are less costly than traditional advertising. Some are free except for your time, others cost pennies per customer. And, they are instantaneous. You can react to changing market conditions, or an overstock, or a competitor's sale instantly. You don't have to wait for the next newspaper to come out.

## INCREASE CUSTOMER LOYALTY

"Turn loyal customers into raving fans. Turn raving fans into product evangelists." This is a common mantra among Internet marketers. Cultivating fans in this way is not applicable to traditional media – it's a phenomenon unique to the Internet due to the dynamics of expression and dialog.

Imagine the benefits of raving fans: lots of referrals, repeat business, and excitement in the press.

# NOTES

Allow customers to express their appreciation of you through social media channels. Foster and encourage contests, competitions, engaging content that elicits comments, fan appreciation events, testimonial campaigns, etc. Loyalty will ensue because your customers will feel heard and appreciated.

## INCREASE PARTICIPANTS IN SOCIAL OR CHARITABLE CAUSES

Social media marketing also facilitates the following: higher level of collaboration, greater momentum in number of participants in social and charitable "causes," quicker awareness in trends, and a more in-depth level of education of your prospects and customers.

## VIRAL EFFECT

What does "viral" mean? Viral refers to something that spreads so quickly that it takes on a life of its own. When a video goes viral, for example, large numbers of people view and share it very quickly.

Sounds like a cash cow, doesn't it? It can be. However, it is a phenomenon that is very difficult to purposefully produce. Everyone wants to be a well-recognized superstar! Every company would love to become a household name! While it's okay to aim high for the viral effect, success comes with persistence and follow through. As with any sales and marketing efforts, it's a numbers game – slow and steady wins the race.

## HIGHER QUALITY OF DIALOG

Unlike traditional static display ads, you can dialogue with your customers and prospects. The benefits of this dialog are obvious: better customer service through listening, more innovations and improvements from customer suggestions, increased loyalty because they see the human side of your business, and customers feel heard and validated.

In traditional advertising, you craft your ad, put it out there, and it is static. You never know who has laid eyes on it, what they thought about your message, or whether they are reacting directly to your message or not. Internet marketing is dynamic. It facilitates immediate feedback through comment and tweet platforms, as well as fan participation. Businesses can also immediately address and respond to individual customers and prospects.

## ABILITY TO REFINE ADVERTISEMENTS AND YOUR MESSAGE

With advanced analytics, you can refine your ads to make them more effective. Track where your traffic is coming from, understand the demographics of your traffic, and really refine and tweak the keywords in your message.

# NOTES

Refining ads that work results in the double benefit of spending advertising dollars more wisely and going deeper into niche demographics more effectively. That is impossible or at least more costly to do in traditional advertising.

## REACH TIGHTLY-DEFINED DEMOGRAPHICS

Narrow your demographics into smaller niches so that you can more effectively craft your marketing message to prospects and customers. People want to know what's in it for them, so talk to them in terms that they identify with and in terms of their passions and specific interests.

Refer to the Demographics exercise in Chapter 4 of this Playbook to narrow down who you want to target, and zero in on that demographic. Shotgun-spray advertising is costly because you are wasting money reaching people who will never buy your product, or benefit from your organization. Reach your exact target niche and you will succeed.

## MANAGE YOUR REPUTATION

True, you cannot completely control your online reputation or what others say about you. However, you can stay in the game and protect your branding. You can be proactive about your online reputation: stay on top of your customer reviews, be aware of how people are talking about you, and address concerns and bad reviews in a timely manner.

Make sure you check your comments and reviews often and respond to them. People other than the one posting the feedback will read your response. Keep it up-to-date. This may sound time consuming, but it's important.

As you can see, many benefits of engaging in online marketing are tangible and measurable. The trick is to have a strategic game plan before you start and stick to your strategic game plan or revise it as you go along. If you pay attention to customer comments, the level of customer engagement, statistics, analytics, and effectiveness of your campaigns, then you will succeed.

# NOTES

# HOW TO MAXIMIZE THE BENEFITS

## IMPROVE SEARCH ENGINE RANKINGS THROUGH KEYWORDS

You can enable prospects to find you more easily through effective Search Engine Optimization (SEO). The first step is by strengthening your keywords.

Keywords are the words that search engines like Google and Bing use to match your website or message to searches someone is conducting. Let's say Mary wants a yoga class. She would probably type yoga classes in St. Paul into the search engine because she lives in St. Paul. She would then get a list of businesses that conduct Yoga classes.

Use good keywords organically (meaning, naturally) in your articles, on your website, and in your descriptions of photos and videos. Do not force them into your content; do not "stuff" your content with the words.

## DEVELOP BACKLINKS TO YOUR WEBSITE FROM OTHER WEBSITES

Another thing you can do, for instance, to get your website ranked better in search results is to find other websites who would be willing to put a link to your website on theirs. You might want to do the same for them. This is called backlinking.

Search engines rate how popular a website is by how many other people validate it by linking to it. The number of visitors and the number of backlinks are two things used in the search engines' formulas to determine how relevant the website or content is to the search.

Backlinks will help your search engine rankings and thus get you more visitors which will move your ranking up even further. "Rank," in this sense, means your website shows up first or on the first page in search results.

## ESTABLISH YOURSELF AS AN EXPERT

When you establish yourself as a leader in your industry you increase your online presence by drawing people to you for advice. People want to associate with those who know what they are doing and are well-respected experts in their fields. The benefits seem obvious: thought-leaders influence decisions (including buying decisions) of large numbers of people.

You can do this by creating original, valuable, and useful content which establishes you as an expert. Change or add to the content frequently so it does not become stale. There is more information on this in the "Content" chapter in this Playbook.

Another way to establish yourself as a thought-leader is to curate others' content and become the expert commentator. You do that by posting thoughtful comments on other websites on the

# **NOTES**

subject you are or want to be considered an expert. Make sure, however, your comments are not frivolous and are professional.

## TRY TO GO VIRAL

Viral marketing is a guerilla marketing technique. The viral effect happens when a video, article, comment, photo or other content reaches a large number of people very quickly.

But how can you try to get your content to go viral? There is no magic formula, but there are measures you can take to increase your chances of going viral:

1. Make sure well-established thought leaders with large numbers of followers see your content. If they like it, they will promote it.
2. Use compelling language and keywords so that people are motivated to "share" and "like" and promote your content.
3. Make it relevant, interesting, or unusual.

Consider outsourcing to professional Internet marketers if you really believe that you have a gem of a video or article for help in making it go viral.

# NOTES

# CHAPTER 4
# FOUNDATIONS

These are the foundations of participating in Internet marketing: demographics, mission statement and listening skills. Make sure these are in place before you launch the platforms discussed in the next section of this Playbook.

# NOTES

# THE DEMOGRAPHICS OF YOUR CUSTOMERS

Of course you have a general idea of what your demographic targets are for prospects and customers. For online marketing, however, you need a very precise and detailed understanding of your demographics. Think of this as advanced market research that is specific to your business. It's target marketing, and it's smart business.

You need to write it down. You need to spell it out. Later, you will refer back to this section.

In traditional marketing, demographics are important. In online marketing, demographics are critical. There are too many choices to be randomly making decisions. You can't throw spaghetti against the wall and see what sticks when it comes to which communities on which you decide to spend precious resources and energy.

While it's true that a dentist could say that any human old enough to have teeth is his/her demographics, the niches need to be teased out: reconstruction, root canals, caps, teenagers, elderly, fillings, check-ups, etc.

## TRY THIS:

Write down your specific demographics. Start with age, gender, income, education level, and geography. Then, try going beyond those basics to drill down further niche groups of shared interests that you can target: hobbies, values (religious, environmental, social, etc.), occupation, means of transportation, dietary preferences, ethnic groups, marital status, renters or homeowners, clothing choices, labor-related activities, habits, pet ownership, political orientation, stage in life, travel preferences and habits, family size, cultural rites of passage (e.g. wedding, graduation), pregnancies, health, technological interests, seasonal habits (tire chains for snow in the mountains, for example), restaurant preferences, holiday behaviors, organization and association affiliations, level of volunteerism, etc.

_____

_____

_____

_____

_____

Don't skip this step. Write it down so that when it's time to decide how to proceed on the Internet, this will be your guide to what communities to seek out and join. You will refer back to this list later.

# **NOTES**

If you are stuck, then do an online search for articles on business demographics or market research. Also, if you are unsure, then think of your best customers or your biggest customers and list everything you know about them.

## INTERMEDIATE CHALLENGE:

The conscious consumer is a passionate demographic of decision makers who make purchases based on their values. Examples: the patients who gravitate towards alternative health care; consumers that want to buy from green companies ("green" means environmentally responsible or sustainable); and those that buy local because of their anti-corporation/pro-entrepreneur stance.

Conscious consumers are highly motivated to be loyal to companies that are in alignment with their values. Conscious consumers can also be powerful allies in terms of referrals – both word of mouth and potential online virility (where "virility" means strength of message, reach, and influence).

Write down the demographics of your customers in terms of value systems: corporate responsibility, Christian or other religious values, environmental responsibility, political orientation, social issues, charitable causes, animal rights, human rights, minimalism and frugality, fair trade and workers' rights, buy American, etc.

_____

_____

_____

_____

_____

Make it easy for the conscious consumer to choose your business by making your mission statement public. Are your values clearly represented in the Mission Statement of your business? Does your business website display your Value Statement and Mission Statement on the About webpage for all to read? Does your brand reflect these values?

There is an excellent article on www.entrepreneur.com, "Targeting the Next Generation," that is worth reading for further information on the younger generation's mentality and values.

# **NOTES**

# MISSION STATEMENT

All effective mission statements have in common critical components that clarify each organization's purpose. When people say, "I'm on a mission," it gives the impression of total, single-minded focus towards a worthwhile goal. Similarly, when an organization composes its official mission, the single-minded focus is narrowed down into a concise statement announcing the worthwhile goal.

Your mission statement is every bit as important as your Business Plan. Write it down! Publish it on your website.

Here's how to write your mission statement and great examples after which to model yours.

Keep in mind your audience: for whom is the mission statement intended? There are different uses and types of mission statements. Some organizations use their mission statement as a publicity tool, others have internal-use only mission statements that serve as a compass for leadership decisions, others publish their mission statements in annual reports meant to be read by investors and potential clients. Knowing your audience is the first step in creating an effective mission statement.

Be clear on your values. Your personal values may overlap with your business values, and that is okay. Make sure that the *values* are clearly stated in the mission statement.

Look for the values incorporated into the following mission statement examples, and the *vision* implied or often explicitly stated.

Non-Profit Statement Example:

"The Jeremiah Program, a broad-based collaborative community initiative, assists low-income mothers and their children to help themselves complete their education and achieve economic self-sufficiency through empowerment skills, access to affordable housing, child development services, health care, support services and meaningful employment. The Jeremiah Program mothers and children develop positive self-esteem and clarify their values on which to build a successful life."

This is a great example of a multi-purpose mission statement. This clarifies the mission of the organization to supporters of the program (charitable donors and volunteers), to potential applicants of the program, to employees, and to the general public.

The values are included skillfully in the statement: collaboration, empowerment, self-sufficiency, family values, and positive self-esteem. The vision is to have single mothers empowered to help themselves get ahead in life while still maintaining focus on family and parenting skills.

# NOTES

Personal Mission Statement Example:

"My mission is to champion others to grow personally, professionally, emotionally and spiritually by using my compassion, my unique perspective, and my belief in others' inherent goodness, integrity, and enormous potential." (This is the author's personal mission statement.)

This statement could be for personal use only, to guide decisions and act as a measuring tool for success, or it could be used for potential clients to be championed.

The values in this statement are leadership as service ("champion others"), compassion, integrity, and faith. The vision is people helping people reach more of their potential through well-rounded growth – personal, professional, emotional, and spiritual.

Business Statement Example:

Here is the Coca-Cola Company's mission statement for Stakeholders which is published in Jeffrey Abrahams' book, *101 Mission Statements From Top Companies* (Ten Speed Press, 2007):

"The Coca-Cola Promise: The Coca-Cola Company exists to benefit and refresh everyone it touches. The basic proposition of our business is simple, solid, and timeless. When we bring refreshment, value, joy and fun to our stakeholders, then we successfully nurture and protect our brands, particularly Coca-Cola. That is the key to fulfilling our ultimate obligation to provide consistently attractive returns to the owners of our business." (p. 40)

The audience for this mission is specifically for the stakeholder.

The values here are stated explicitly: refreshment, value, joy, fun, and attractive returns. These words were obviously carefully chosen by those who crafted this mission statement. The "ultimate obligation" of "attractive returns" is a powerful way to state the company's vision and keeps the values stated in context.

A separate mission statement is published on The Coca-Cola Company's website for access by the general public:

"Everything we do is inspired by our enduring mission:
- To Refresh the World… in body, mind, and spirit.
- To Inspire Moments of Optimism… through our brands and our actions.
- To Create Value and Make a Difference… everywhere we engage."

These values are consistent with the stakeholder version of the mission: refreshment and value are echoed in addition to inspiration.

# **NOTES**

## TRY THIS:

Write your Mission Statement. It can be a sentence, or a paragraph. Remember to include your values explicitly.

_____

_____

_____

_____

_____

## INTERMEDIATE CHALLENGES:

1. Write out your Vision Statement. The vision is the "ideal world, the ideal state." Again, this can be a sentence (e.g. "Our vision is to have the company name a household word.") or a paragraph.

_____

_____

_____

_____

_____

2. Write a separate Mission Statement for your sales team. You can ask them to help craft the mission, or you can propose one to them as a motivator to accomplish the mission!

_____

_____

_____

_____

_____

# NOTES

# LISTENING SKILLS AND HUMILITY

Listening to conversations online about your business and your industry is a critical part of your online marketing strategy. Remember, we are not flinging spaghetti against the wall to see what sticks. Listening will help you take the temperature of your prospects. Listening will ground you in reality.

Have humility when you approach Internet marketing. Normally, you push out your message in traditional advertising. The message is static and under your control. With Internet marketing, you pull prospects toward you, enticing them to come to you when they are ready.

Humility will serve you as you realize that your prospects and customers have feelings, ideas, and free will. People do not want to be pushed into doing business with you. They want to be pulled, enticed, seduced.

Unlike traditional TV commercials, for example, where you announce that you are the best in the whole world for what you do, online marketing is more subtle and requires humility.

Authenticity and humility go hand in hand, here. Be authentic! The Internet makes everything and everyone transparent. You will find that humility will serve you in being authentic. Be honest about your business. Show your human side.

## TRY THIS:

Sign up for Google Alerts by going to http://www.google.com/alerts so that you can receive notifications when others are blogging or posting reviews about you or your business. You can sign up for multiple keywords and key phrases by entering them as "search queries."

You will receive email updates whenever Google discovers your keywords mentioned on other websites. This is a great listening activity and a great way to monitor your reputation.

# SECTION II
# PLATFORMS, TOOLS
# AND TACTICS

# NOTES

# PLATFORMS AND TOOLS

## WHAT IS THE DIFFERENCE BETWEEN PLATFORMS, TOOLS, AND TACTICS?

A platform is a stage upon which you stand to deliver your message. Platforms are often websites or sometimes categories of websites that enable you to get the word out about your business. You need a platform upon which to convey your message, your brand, and your character. You need platforms upon which to hold conversations and manage comments.

The ten platforms we will learn in this section of the Playbook are the following:
1. Website
2. Facebook
3. YouTube
4. Twitter
5. LinkedIn
6. Google+
7. Daily Deals & Check-in Sites
8. Blogs and Vlogs
9. Event Promotions and Meetup Sites
10. Online Directories and Reviews

Beginners and even intermediate players of online marketing will have ample time to work through the challenges for each platform. This Playbook will walk you through the platforms one at a time so that you can become comfortable and familiar with them at your own pace. To begin with, just choose two or three – don't try and master all ten!

# NOTES

Tools, on the other hand, are what put the wind in the sails to the platforms. We will explore the tools, but in less depth, in the chapter following the platforms.

Tools increase the effectiveness of the content on your platforms just as oil enables the cogs to turn in a machine. Tools make the job of engagement easier, less time consuming, and less costly – especially when it comes to doing the marketing yourself.

A tool is a thing you *use* to make the job easier. A tactic, on the other hand, is a thing that you *do*. You employ tactics to achieve results (and the results you shoot for are guided by your strategy).

Examples of tools (things you *use*) are as follows:
> Automatic Posting Tools - Hootsuite
> Facebook Applications
> Website Analytics
> Affiliate Programs
> Webinars, Classes, eBooks, DVDs
> Sophisticated opt-ins/ad copy

Examples of tactics (things you *do*) are as follows:
> Search Engine Optimization (SEO)
> Webinar Swaps
> Social Bookmarking
> E-Mail Campaigns
> Ad Campaigns (PPC, etc.)
> Content Leveraging
> Professional Branding
> Phone Applications – tactic to reach mobile users
> Blog Monetization
> Creating Viral Content – tactic to increase reach
> Offering a DVD or E-Book

This is not a comprehensive list of tools and tactics. There are many ways to increase your effectiveness when using the platforms. You should also know your limits when it comes to learning curve and time investment for implementing these tools and tactics yourself versus hiring an expert or professional in any of these areas.

See Chapter 2: Tools and Tactics, below, for expanded explanations of tools and tactics.

# NOTES

# CHAPTER 5
# PLATFORMS

This chapter will take ten platforms and give you things to try and challenges to work through so that you can be comfortable using them to achieve your business goals. Go at your own pace, within your own comfort zone. Remember, you only have to work with two or three to begin with so that you don't get overwhelmed or spread yourself too thin.

*A note about passwords...*

There is a space to write down your login and password information for each platform in their respective sections. However, if you do not feel comfortable doing this, there is a **Master Password List** in the Appendix.

# NOTES

# WEBSITES

Website address: _____

Domain host name: _____

(The "domain" is who you pay to host your website. Wordpress is free, for example.)

Domain password: _____

(What is the password to get into your website if you want to make changes or edit it?)

While your website does not have to be the hub of your online presence (although it usually is the main hub), it is a place where you can exert the most control over your message, your branding and your business character. The website is where most companies host their shopping cart, field comments and allow customers to contact them, and often contains the blog. Websites also build trust and can generate quality leads.

Often, the first thing a person does when looking for a business or an organization is to search the Internet for a website. Studies have shown that most consumers today select the place they shop, the restaurant they will go to, a vacation rental or the flight they book by going to a website.

In terms of demographics, those under 30 years old view businesses without a website unfavorably. They may think you are too new, not technologically savvy, or that you are not credible.

A website can help you with the following:

- Credibility
- Building customer trust
- Lead generation (if you optimize it with an offer or a newsletter that gathers emails)
- Sales (shopping cart)
- Search engine ranking

Just as professional speakers know the importance of having a clear purpose of their speech, so you must be very clear on the purpose of your website. Is the purpose of your website simply to establish credibility? Are you selling an eBook, DVD, video, training course, or products? Is the purpose of your website to capture leads for an eNewsletter or autoresponder sequence? Do you want to increase customer trust, reduce attrition, or educate current customers and prospects? Is the purpose of your website to encourage customer engagement with an active forum, discussion threads and comments? Or, perhaps you have another purpose? Think this through.

# NOTES

Write down the purpose of your website:

_____

_____

_____


## WEBSITE ARCHITECTURE

The architecture of your website lets visitors find their way around the website (navigation). If your website is not navigation-friendly, then visitors will likely get frustrated and leave.

Refer back to the purpose of your website. This will guide you through making sure your navigation makes sense and is clean and straightforward.

There are two types of sites: The first type is informational--it simply provides information about who you are, what you do, and where you are located. The second type actually allows a customer to buy a product or order a service online from your site. This type of website will also need a shopping cart.

At a minimum, your website should have the following individual web pages:

- **Home** - This page should always be on left-most side if horizontal, or on top if vertical.
- **About** - This page describes what your company does, a brief bio of the principals, and history. This is usually a tab right next to the Home page tab. "About" could include information about your team members, as well. Here is where you can publish your Mission Statement.
- **Products** - This page is where you list and describe what you are offering or selling. If you are selling a product, list it, or all that you sell with a well-keyworded description, and prices. Include pictures. Remember to list benefits as well as features. Be diligent about SEO (search engine optimization) opportunities, and don't be stingy when it comes to details and descriptions.
- **Services** - If you are offering a service instead of or in addition to selling products, describe that service or all the services you offer. If possible, list a price. If not, instruct them to call or e-mail for a quote.
- **Contact** - This mandatory page enables customers and prospects to reach you for questions, to enlist your business or for customer support. Remember to include **Hours** even though you also want the hours listed on the home page (if applicable). This webpage is where you can add a link to Google maps if you are a brick and mortar business.

# NOTES

You might break some of your information into separate pages. Examples of additional pages:

- Blog
- Industry information
- Calendar or Events if you are a speaker or hold frequent events
- News
- Resources
- FAQ (Frequently Asked Questions)
- New patient forms
- Treatment methods
- Schedule of classes

## TRY THIS:

Write down the tabs for your website below:

**Home About** _____ _____ _____ _____ _____ **Contact**

## INTERMEDIATE CHALLENGES:

1. Craft a more comprehensive schematic of your website architecture by making an outline of subpages:

**Home About** _____ _____ _____ _____ _____ **Contact**

Subpages: _____ _____ _____ _____ _____

_____ _____ _____ _____ _____

_____ _____ _____ _____ _____

2. Write notes here for elements that you would like to add to your website to improve the visitor experience and increase their trust levels (e.g. sophisticated guest book or place for visitors to post comments, adding a shopping cart).

_____

_____

_____

_____

# NOTES

## MOBILE WEBSITES

The viewing experience is different on a mobile site versus a traditional website. Even if you do not use your mobile phone or a mobile device to access the Internet, your customers and prospects are. Remember, this is not about your habits of using the Internet. It's about *theirs*.

According to Google research, over 70% of consumers want mobile friendly websites. Also, recent data shows that 57% of local Internet search is performed on mobile devices. These numbers are only growing.

The new websites being built today are called "responsive" because they respond to the various screen sizes that users use today, from a smartphone to an iPad and all the way up to a large desktop PC monitor.

For small businesses that can't afford a new website, you can purchase a mobile site. It's a completely separate website that when mobile users click on your website, they are automatically taken to your mobile site.

Here are important aspects of a mobile website:

1. **Click to Call:** the ability to call you with the push of a button.
2. **Click for Maps:** be able to find your business and get directions easily.
3. **Business Hours:** can they visit you immediately?
4. **About Us:** be able to see what exactly you do or sell.
5. **Thumb-Sized Buttons:** links and navigation buttons that are easy to access and user-friendly.
6. **Large Text:** the number one problem of websites that aren't mobile-friendly, is the inability to read the text without pinching and zooming. A mobile websites makes all text large and easy to read.

## TRY THIS:

Check your website from an iPhone or another smartphone. Is yours viewable without having to use your fingers to zoom in? Is critical information immediately available: hours, phone, and directions?

Mobile websites must be set up for simplicity of use. They must allow for fingertip operation—sliding or tapping. They should also integrate with social media sites like Facebook, Twitter, and LinkedIn. They also must load fast.

# NOTES

## CONTENT: ARTICLES AND VIDEOS

Content is a general word that describes the form in which you put your message. On your website, you can tell your story or message in an article, in a video, or a blog entry.

Your website should contain concise information that will help the customer or prospect find what they are looking for. The content will include some static information about products and services, as well as updated and fresh content as your industry and your business grow and evolve.

It's very important that the information on your website is up-to-date. Even when you make a small change in your business, such as the hours of operation, update that change on your website right away. This is important for credibility and also usefulness to the consumer.

You also want to ensure that your website is very professional in both the content and the overall design. Check the content carefully to be sure there are no misspellings, typos or grammatical errors. If you are sloppy on the look and language of your website, then you send a message that you are probably sloppy with your business and customer service.

# NOTES

# FACEBOOK

Date Facebook Fan Page created: _____

Facebook email login: _____

(The email that you used to sign up for Facebook.)

Facebook password: _____

Names of Administrators: _____

(You can authorize more than one person to allow them to post as administrators on your time-line.)

Facebook is the #2 most viewed website in the world, second only to Google English. Don't delude yourself into thinking that your customer demographics are not using Facebook. Don't excuse yourself from engaging with Facebook users because you don't understand how businesses can appropriately use this online platform.

If you do not already have a Facebook business page, you should block out 60 – 90 minutes to just sit down and create your page. It's self-explanatory; you just have to be patient with the process. Look for a tutorial on YouTube if you are unsure on how to begin. Or, hire a social media tutor like Joyce Feustel of Denver, CO to walk you through the setup process. See resources in the Appendix.

Facebook helps you with the following:

- Brand awareness
- R & D (research and development)
- Increasing customer loyalty
- Reputation management
- Lead generation
- Customer service management
- Better quality dialog with customers and prospects

Make sure that you are very clear about the reason you are using Facebook in your online marketing strategy. Don't use Facebook just because others say you should: be clear about your reasons so that when you plan your posts, they are purposeful and productive.

# <u>NOTES</u>

## TRY THIS:

Choose from the bulleted list above and highlight your main reasons for using Facebook. Write below any notes, thoughts, ideas, or tactics.

_____

_____

_____

_____

## FACEBOOK FANS

Facebook is a way to reach out to your fans so that you can turn loyal customers into raving fans and raving fans into product (or service) evangelists. This is a space for you to listen to your prospects and customers. Really listen to your fans. Facebook is a two-way street of communication.

If you are posting content on your business Facebook business page but you have no fans (represented by how many people have clicked "like" for the page), then you have missed the point. With very few fans, you are posting in a void – even if you are posting valuable content, interesting links and announcements.

Invite your friends, family, and customers to click "like" on your Facebook business page. Add a link to your Facebook page in the signature of your business email. Add a link to your website, too.

## TRY THIS:

Below, write down tactics you might use to increase your number of fans (e.g. hire a Facebook for businesses expert to launch and manage a Facebook ad campaign, or create and promote a professional opt-in – a free promotional offer to fans who click "like" and enter their email):

_____

_____

_____

_____

# NOTES

Don't spend money on buying Facebook fans. This is wasted money. You want quality fans that are truly fans or prospects, not fake ones so that your numbers look good. An oft quoted social media mantra states: "Don't count fans and followers like you count bottle caps."

Remember, it's both quantity and quality. You want quality fans and a good number of them. You want to post quality announcements and a good number of them. Slow and steady wins the race when it comes to building a following on Facebook or any of the social media platforms.

There really are no shortcuts to building a following, just as there are no shortcuts to marketing and encouraging word of mouth referrals.

In the **tear-out sheets** at the back of this book there are pages where you can track your progress on increasing your number of Facebook fans.

## POSTING ON FACEBOOK

Intuitively, you already know that it is inappropriate to post self-centered announcements and inordinate promotional-type posts. Everything in moderation is a good rule of thumb to go by when it comes to etiquette about posting.

On the other hand, do not avoid promotional posts like the plague. Yes, customers DO want to hear about what is going on with your business. Just do it in moderation.

What to Post and What Not to Post

So, what types of posts are appropriate for a business Facebook Fan Page?

Two rules of thumb:

1. Variety is the spice of life.
2. Post content or links to content that are either educational or entertaining (when appropriate).

As a reference, here are more types of posts and ways to engage your fans using Facebook:

- Events. List your events. Sales events are okay, but you can also list PR events, Open Houses, classes, and more.
- Polls. Ask engaging questions, not just market research questions of your fans.
- Photos. Post photos of events, photos of fans, photos of owners and employees.
- Videos. People love videos, so videos are extremely popular and have the most potential to "go viral," but make sure that they are appropriate and inoffensive.
- Trivia. Post trivia questions that people care about (not, "what year did our store open?") related to your business or industry.
- YouTube. Add a link to your YouTube channel right on your Facebook page. Promote your own videos as well as others.

# NOTES

In the **tear-out sheets** at the back of this book there are pages to track your posts and write down your goals. Be sure to fill it out regularly.

## INTERMEDIATE CHALLENGE:

Write down sources (e.g. websites and books) of inspirational or educational content that you might post or share with your Facebook fans. Here are some examples: well-recognized industry resources, associations, industry leaders, reference books, and YouTube channels.

_____

_____

_____

_____

## FACEBOOK ADS

Do not worry for now about placing Facebook ads unless you have an event you want to promote, or a product (like an e-book or DVD) to sell.

Running ad campaigns online is great because you can tightly control the budget (down to a maximum number of dollars per day you want to spend). However, consider outsourcing to a Facebook professional or investing the time to read up on how to run a formal Facebook ad campaign before launching into this area.

Facebook does have incredible potential for increasing reach ("reach," in this case, means getting your message out to an increasing number of people). There are lots of applications and sophisticated ways to use Facebook for business. Just make sure that you are using this platform in an orchestrated manner in conjunction with your other platforms (e.g. your website) so that your activities are purposeful.

## FACEBOOK APPLICATIONS

Adding applications to your Facebook page is for intermediate and advanced Internet marketers. If you feel that you are ready to add applications, then try using websites like AvenueSocial. com or ShortStack.com that have wizards to walk you through creating applications. Otherwise, outsource to a social media company that specializes in Facebook for businesses.

What kinds of applications are available? Examples of great uses:

• Enable commerce
• Run a contest or sweepstake

# NOTES

- Allow customers to check in (announce that they are in your place of business)
- Provide navigation and interactive maps
- Act as a landing page for a coupon or other offer
- Point to YouTube videos
- Games
- Voting or sharing promotions
- Newsletter integration
- eBook download offer

Only spend money on applications or ad campaigns when you can justify it in your formal marketing budget. Stick to the strategy that you create (see Strategy in Section III: Chapter 1 for help on creating your Online Marketing Plan). Be clear on why you are spending the money and what your expected ROI is for that activity.

# NOTES

# YOUTUBE

YouTube channel name: _____

Login email: _____

Login password: _____

The Jan. 30, 2012 issue of *Time Magazine* has a 4-page article about YouTube, calling it "the billion-eyed beast." According to Time, YouTube "gets 4 billion page views a day, which adds up to 1 trillion a year." Imagine, now, almost two years later, how that viewership has grown.

YouTube is a website where anyone can post videos for others to view. YouTube is the third most-viewed website in the world, behind Google English and Facebook. It is the second biggest search engine (yes, even bigger than Yahoo or Bing), even though it only searches videos.

Your demographics use YouTube. The videos are not *only* silly, inane, amateur clips of stupid animal tricks. You might be surprised to find out about the educational and interesting videos to watch!

Watch how-to videos, watch informative lectures on science and other topics, watch inspiring videos, watch creative videos that fans of companies have created, and lots more on YouTube. This platform can be very useful to both consumer and business owner if used properly.

Yes, businesses can effectively use YouTube. It's a great platform to create and store content (video content, of course), as well as a great way to curate others' video content that is pertinent to your business and educational to your customers.

Use videos as a tool to reach those with a short attention span and have no time or interest in reading articles.

YouTube can help you with the following:
- Brand Awareness
- Search engine results
- Driving traffic to your shopping cart
- Building customer trust
- Establishing thought leadership

Use this platform to help you with SEO (search engine optimization). Videos with well-written descriptions rank over 50 times better in search engine results than well-keyworded blog articles or web pages. Videos have the potential for reaching a wider audience than articles.

# NOTES

## SETTING UP A YOUTUBE CHANNEL

A YouTube account is called a channel. If you do not have one set up for your business or organization, you can do so for free. Set one up, now. This way, when you are ready to launch a video marketing campaign (such as a series of customer testimonials or video tours of your business), then you have the channel ready to go.

Remember to record your channel name, email used to sign up (usually a gmail address), and password. Use the space above or write it on your **Master Password List** found at the back of the book.

## TYPES OF VIDEOS AND VIDEO CAMPAIGNS

Appropriate types of videos for businesses to post on YouTube include the following: **educational** (product, general industry tips, how to, etc.), **entertaining** (when appropriate), coverage of events to evidence success and popularity, interviews, and testimonials.

Do NOT create a commercial. Viewers do not want to watch you talk about yourself or how great your business is. Remember: videos must be either educational or entertaining. While it's okay to have a short (30 seconds or less) video giving a tour of your business if it's important to raise the comfort level of first timers (a good example of this is chiropractors' offices), stay clear of blatant commercials.

Remember when creating testimonial videos to make them engaging and interesting. There are far too many videos that are bland, static, generic, forced and boring. If it is not interesting, do not post it!

Also remember to obtain *signed and dated media release forms* from all persons in the video, regardless of age. You can get free templates for the media release forms online.

You can create your own videos or hire a professional, but it's always up to you to decide what types of videos are appropriate for your business by using common sense and adhering to your values and business mission.

## VIDEO PRODUCTION QUALITY

Viewers are very forgiving when it comes to quality of videos. You can shoot them from your iPhone, from your digital camera, or even from your webcam. There are free editing software programs available (e.g. Windows Movie Maker) that you can download and quickly figure out how to do the following:

1. Add scrolling credits at the end.
2. Link to your website or commentary at the bottom of the screen during your video.
3. Edit by deleting sections, splicing, etc.
4. Add fun special effects.
5. Add music or other sound track.

# <u>NOTES</u>

Hire Coach Angela to help you with strategies and tactics for YouTube, or hire a social media expert. Do not budget for a professional videographer unless you are either bartering or are very clear on your ROI for the project you are shooting. Yes, creating a professional DVD that you might market – that's something that would warrant a professional videographer, for example.

## TRY THIS:

YouTube is a grossly underused platform for business, but you would benefit greatly from searching for competitors videos and other industry videos to learn what is already being done, what is being done well, and what videos are missing or lacking that you can create.

Set aside a half hour to search for videos on YouTube, putting yourself in your customers' shoes. Would they search for how-to videos, informational videos about your product, demonstration videos, or other information?

Write down the date and time that you commit to browsing YouTube. Or, do it right now.

Date: _____        Time: _____

Below, make notes on searches you performed, results, ideas, and thoughts.

_____

_____

_____

_____

## INTERMEDIATE CHALLENGE:

What type of video campaign could you launch to generate some excitement around your brand? List ideas, here. Don't forget to list video footage of events that your business hosts or participates in throughout the year.

_____

_____

# NOTES

# TWITTER

Twitter username: _____

Twitter password: _____

Often maligned as a useless mass texting tool to announce what you had for breakfast, Fortune 500 companies successfully use Twitter to manage customer service with more speed and less cost.

Twitter is an excellent search tool for listening to conversations. It can also be part of your branding, helping with consistency of brand across all online platforms. You can also announce your events on Twitter as an effective promotion tool, once you get some critical mass with your followers.

But what is Twitter, exactly? It is a platform – a stage upon which you stand to deliver your message. Twitter allows for very short messages: 140 characters at a maximum. Characters include letters, punctuation, and spaces.

Social media experts call using Twitter "micro-blogging." This is a fancy way to say that you are blogging in very short messages.

Remember, as with other platforms, you can either compose your own content or you can use Twitter to curate content. When you curate content, it means that you sift through lots of information out there and choose what you think is the best of the best and pass it along to your followers. Followers trust you, then, as the place to go for good info about your industry.

This social media platform can help you with the following:
- Better customer service
- Increased customer trust
- Brand awareness
- Credibility
- Reputation management
- Better quality dialog with customers and prospects
- Event announcements

# NOTES

## SETTING UP YOUR TWITTER ACCOUNT

If you do not have a Twitter account, it is easy and free to set one up. Go to www.twitter.com and sign up.

Take the time to fill out your profile: upload a picture, type a 160-character bio, and a link to your company's website. According to Dan Zarrella's *The Science of Marketing*, "…accounts that provide a picture, bio, and home page link [link to your company's website] all have more followers than accounts that do not." (p. 59-60)

Identify yourself as an expert or authority in your field when filling out your profile. Zarrella's data shows that you will be more likely to gain more followers if you are perceived as an expert.

Find free Twitter tutorials online, and in less than one hour the sharp-minded and determined business owner will understand the huge potential to reach tightly-defined demographics quickly. Do a search on YouTube for a video tutorial by typing "Twitter tutorial" in the search bar.

Basic tutorials will also explain how to use hashtags (the "#" symbol) for marking a keyword, how to conduct multiple types of searches on Twitter, how to talk directly to Twitter users (if you type "@" in front of a person's Twitter identity, you speak directly to that person and show up in their Twitter feed and will be seen by all of their followers), and how to jump in conversations already rapidly firing.

Also, you can find tutorials on how to customize the graphics for your Twitter account (uploading the correct image size for your background). This is one area where you might consider hiring a graphic designer to insure that your branding and images are consistent across all your online marketing platforms.

Gaining followers is as easy as you initiating the act of following people and then engaging in their conversations using the "@" symbol and the "#." Generally speaking, if you offer value and interesting comments, others will follow you back.

## TWITTER AND YOUR BRANDING

Twitter can help with your company's branding in three ways: graphics are consistent; hashtag campaigns are catchy, clear, and consistent; and messaging and tweets are consistent with your brand.

Consistent graphics are important in your branding efforts online. So make sure the graphics on your Twitter page look good and are properly visible in the background. If you cannot figure this out, hire a graphic designer or look on www.fiverr.com for help with this for only $5 or $10.

Social media experts recommend that you create a hashtag (this is the hashtag symbol: "#") with a keyword for your business. In addition to your username (for Twitter, your username is called a "handle"), a consistent keyword can be useful for both Twitter and Google+.

# NOTES

Here are some examples of #keywords:

1.  Red Bull, an energy drink company, has been very successful in its social media reach ("reach" is the number of people that see your message). Red Bull has 1.2 million followers on Twitter and 40.8 million likes on Facebook (as of November, 2013).

    Twitter handle: @redbull

    #keyword: #givesyouwings

    Notice that when you use the hashtag, you do not put a space between the words. It's not #gives you wings. Nor is it #gives #you #wings. It's #givesyouwings. The slogan "gives you wings" is used in their TV and radio commercials, and is a recognizable part of Red Bull's branding.

2.  A chiropractor might want to use something catchy: #chiromagic or #spinefix.

3.  A realtor might be creative: #myfirsthouse or #proudhomeowner.

4.  An IT (information technology) guy might use #IThelp or #fixitfast.

5.  A carpet cleaner company might use #cleancarpet or #carpetexperts.

## TRY THIS:

Following others is the first step to participating in Twitter. Here are two things that you can play with to get better acquainted with this platform and to grow your presence.

1. Spend 20 minutes searching Twitter for keywords. In the Twitter search bar, type a keyword that you are interested in: "#recycling," or "#LEED," or "#green construction" for examples. Then, follow Twitter users that you think are making interesting tweets. They may follow you back. There is a tear-out sheet in the Appendix for you to track your number of followers over time.

Write down the date and time that you commit to a 20-minute search session on Twitter. Or, do it right now.

Date: _____        Time: _____

2. Make a list, below, of the following:

*   Brand ambassadors (your biggest fans and happy customers)
*   Industry leaders and colleagues (thought leaders with lots of influence)
*   Competitors (direct and indirect)

# NOTES

| Name or company | Number of Followers |
|---|---|
| _____ | _____ |
| _____ | _____ |
| _____ | _____ |
| _____ | _____ |
| _____ | _____ |
| _____ | _____ |

Now look up these people and companies on Twitter and follow them. Make a note of how many followers they have, how often they are tweeting, and what kind of content they are tweeting.

## INTERMEDIATE CHALLENGE:

1. When you create an editorial calendar (for more information about creating an editorial calendar, see the **Content** chapter in Section III of this Playbook), carve out just five minutes a day to log in to Twitter and follow other Twitter users.

Don't begin tweeting until you have followers. Sending out messages in a void is a waste of time. If a tree falls in a forest with no one to hear, does it make a sound? Yes, it makes a sound, but there is no one to hear it. You can tweet, but what good does it do if there is no one to hear it? You can tweet for practice, but don't go overboard until you have gained momentum in number of followers.

Use the Twitter tear-out sheet in the appendix to record your progress with this platform.

## INCREASING YOUR EXPOSURE ON TWITTER

Here are some tips on how to increase your reach on Twitter.

1.  Tweet. Your followers will stay engaged if you engage with them. Remember out of sight, out of mind. Every day you should tweet something of interest about your business or organization. According to Zarrella, data shows that there is no such thing as over-tweeting.
2.  Increase your followers. One way is by inviting everyone you know to follow you. Put a

# NOTES

Twitter link on your website. Put your Twitter handle on all printed material, and display it in your place of business or office lobby.

3. Follow others. Every day, you will find suggested followers on Twitter. Follow people or organizations that you think might be interested in your business, your organization, or in you. Usually half of the people you randomly follow will follow you back.

4. Send private tweets to your followers. While data shows that in the case of Twitter, engagement does not necessarily increase reach, it is important to engage in conversation (by using the "@" symbol to directly address someone). Only do this if you have something meaningful to add to the conversation.

5. From time to time, look at who is following you, look to see who is following them. Follow some of those people. In other words. Look at who is following your followers and who is following those you are following. Read their profiles, tweets, and see how many followers they have (as an indication of their influence) to figure out whether or not you want to follow them. Again, they may follow you back and it spirals outwards from there.

## WHAT TO TWEET

A tweet is a 140-character message that you send on Twitter. What should you send?

Remember to change it up. Variety and relevance are the keys to success. Here are some suggestions:

- Inspirational quotes
- Announcements
- Events
- Photos. Make sure you own the copyright.
- Links to interesting content (videos, articles, etc.)
- Messages directly to other Twitter users

Use the **tear-out sheets** at the end of this book to track your progress

# <u>NOTES</u>

# LINKEDIN

LinkedIn account name: _____

LinkedIn password: _____

LinkedIn is another website like Facebook and Twitter where you can connect with potential customers or people who would have an interest in your organization or business. LinkedIn is a place where people network online.

Mostly, LinkedIn is for B2B (business to business) instead of B2C (business to consumer). Also, some companies look on LinkedIn for public resumes when they are hiring for additional staff.

Use this platform for the following:

- B2B online networking
- Resume posting/credibility
- Establish thought leadership
- Increase search engine results (SEO)
- Recruiting employees
- Industry visibility

You can learn how to use LinkedIn in about two hours or so, once you sit down and apply yourself to learning your way around the platform. This is a great way to extend your reach and make more connections with other professionals.

The best use of LinkedIn is to fill out the profile as thoroughly as possible and begin making connections. Remember, you have a profile for yourself, as do each of the employees of your company who are on LinkedIn. You also should have a company page for your business, which can be managed by you and selected members of your staff. Having a personal profile and company page that are filled out will add positively to your overall reputation management and provide more SEO opportunities for your company website.

Therefore, your personal profile and your business profile on LinkedIn will help increase your overall online presence. Participating in LinkedIn groups is a great way to establish visibility and credibility in your industry. Thought leaders answer questions, post intriguing polls and questions, and discuss topics in others' posts.

You should make it a habit to revisit LinkedIn on occasion. Schedule 10 – 15 minutes twice a month in your editorial calendar (for more information about creating an editorial calendar, see

# NOTES

the **Content** chapter in Section III of this Playbook). You can maximize this platform by doing the following:

- Making recommendations. A recommendation is a professional testimonial by colleagues or by customers.
- Asking for recommendations. You want happy colleagues, contractors and customers to leave good recommendations for you.
- Endorsing others. You can endorse others' skills if you have done business with them.
- Asking others to endorse your skills. Part of filling out your profile includes taking the time to list all of the skills at which you are good.

## SETTING UP YOUR LINKEDIN ACCOUNT

Go ahead, now, and set up your free personal LinkedIn account if you have not already done so. Carve out an hour of your time to sit down and fill everything out. Be mindful of key words for your skills and your industry, and what is specific to your business.

## TRY THIS:

Write down the date and time that you commit to filling out your LinkedIn profile. Or, do it right now.

Date: _____        Time: _____

Remember, LinkedIn is simply a virtual networking tool. It's not a selling tool. It's not a marketing tool. LinkedIn is all about professional networking.

## INTERMEDIATE CHALLENGES:

1. Now, create a LinkedIn company page for your business. Hover your mouse over the "interests" tab on the top row of tabs. Now, click on "companies." Then, click on "Add a Company" link on the upper right corner of the screen.

You must have a valid email address that is through your company's website, or you cannot set up a LinkedIn business page. If you use yahoo, or gmail, or any other email not through your website, you will be unable to set up the company profile.

Be sure to fill out the products section (found to the immediate right of the home tab on the pages menu bar) as fully as possible. This way, your connections can make good recommendations for your services and products. Also, it's good to have nice pictures that are current and attractive for your company page.

# <u>NOTES</u>

2. Play around with filtering your news feed by doing the following:

When on your home page in LinkedIn, look to the upper right corner of your updates news feed. Hover your mouse over the "All Updates" button that has a tiny arrow next to it and filter your updates news feed by either "profiles" or "shares."

Use the "like," "share," and "comment" buttons to participate on others' profiles by encouraging them.

Use the **tear-out sheet** in the back of the book to track your progress over time with this platform.

# NOTES

# GOOGLE+

Google account name: _____

Google password: _____

You can make posts on your Google+ personal or business page, just as you make posts on your Facebook personal or business page. Just as you can "like" and "share" something on Facebook, you can "+1" (similar to "like) and "share" on Google+.

Google+ is part of Google. Logging on or signing in is easy, since it's the same for all Google platforms: YouTube, gmail, Google+, Google maps, and Google calendar.

Google+ is a rich platform that offers a feed, circles of friends that you control, hangouts for video conferences, and event promotion. Remember to keep your branding (images and messages) consistent, just as you do with all of the other platforms.

## GOOGLE+ CIRCLES

One of the interesting differences between Google+ and Facebook is that Google lets you create "circles" of friends so that you can selectively post or announce on your Google+ "feed" (which is similar to your "timeline" on Facebook). Circles are created and controlled by you. For example, you have a circle of friends from church that you don't necessarily want to be seeing what you are posting to your hunting or poker buddies. So, you have a circle for poker buddies, and a separate circle for church friends. When you make a post that is poker-related, you only share it with the poker buddies circle of friends.

You can create any number of circles and put your friends in one or multiple circles: you can have a circle for business colleagues, a circle for family members, a poker buddies circle, a hunting circle, and a circle for acquaintances. This is just an example.

Have a little fun with your business circles by drilling down hyper-niche demographics. Create circles for people that fall into each demographic. Again, if there is overlap, you can place people in multiple circles. This way, you control the messages in your posts to tailor them exactly to your hyper-niche audience.

## GOOGLE+ HANGOUTS

Google+ also has "hangouts" which is a live way to talk to multiple people with webcams. It's kind of like a webinar, but everyone can be on camera. A hangout is like a group webcam conference call. You can use them for personal reasons, or you can use them for business meetings, conferences, and educational sessions.

# <u>NOTES</u>

A great feature of Google+ hangouts is that your videos, unless otherwise restricted, are posted to YouTube so that you can see them later. This gives posterity to the videos, and gives you the chance to extend your reach with the content.

Some hangouts are huge, and people can watch them that are not in the inner circle of those participating. This also increases your reach, and lends to the possibility of the video achieving the viral effect.

## GOOGLE+ EVENTS

When people RSVP for Google+ events, it shows up automatically on their Google calendar, if they are using that. This is really slick, as the younger generation often use community calendars to coordinate with colleagues, friends, and family.

Google+ events is on the checklist of websites on which you should post your events to promote them online. See the checklist in the Appendix B.

## GOOGLE COMMUNITIES

Just as Facebook has groups, and LinkedIn has groups, so Google+ has communities for different interest groups. Find communities that already exist that are in alignment with your values and your business or industry and join them. You can also create a community to generate discussion and buzz around topics that affect your business.

Participation in communities can be fun, and a way to make new friends for your personal and business Google+ profiles. It's also a great way to keep up on industry news and current events related to that topic.

## SETTING UP YOUR GOOGLE+ ACCOUNT

As with Twitter and Facebook, it's important to keep images consistent in your branding. Make sure that your graphics look good in the banner, as well as images that you post.

To set up your Google+ account, go to https://plus.google.com and either create an account or sign in with your gmail login information.

Use Google+ in your branding along with your Twitter campaign. Google+ is now enabling you to use # (refer to the **Twitter** section, above, for more information about using the hashtag symbol) with keywords. The #keywords are now much more searchable than ever before.

# NOTES

**TRY THIS:**

1. Spend a little time on Google+ and find out if any of your friends or acquaintances are using it. It's a social platform, just like Facebook. The more you and your friends use it, the more you get out of it. You can also see what your friends and colleagues are interested in as they "+1" (similar to a "like" on Facebook) an interesting item on the Internet.

2. You can also click "+1" on items that you think others would be interested in.

**INTERMEDIATE/ADVANCED CHALLENGE:**

If you use Google adwords for Pay Per Click (PPC) campaigns, you should use Google+ to enhance the click through rate.

Do a YouTube search for "Google+ and adwords" to find tutorials on how to enhance your current campaign.

# NOTES

# DAILY DEALS AND CHECK-IN SITES

Daily deals serve as a means to offer coupons… online. Check-ins serve as a means to offer coupons or track the number of times loyal customers come to your business. They are also a great way to display your company's popularity.

Check-in sites like Foursquare and Facebook allow your customers to announce to their friends that they are at your place of business – they are "checking in." This is an immediate, real-time announcement: "I'm here at Joe's Pizzeria having lunch with my girlfriend."

Customers can also post reviews of your business on the check-in sites.

There is some debate as to the value of daily deals such as Groupon, Living Social, and other popular mobile (cell phone-based) applications. The reason for this is because business owners have complained that the customers that cash in on the deep discounts offered through the daily deals are not their normal demographics, that the customers do not seem to come back after the deal, and that their regular customers cash in on the deal, as well.

However, there are appropriate uses of daily deals:
- Quick cash infusion for the business (even if it is just a one-time offer)
- Clever use of a loss-leader if the employees are properly trained to up-sell to the customers once they walk in the door
- As a tool for customer appreciation
- Brand awareness

If you choose to offer a deep discount for a daily deal website, you should hire a coach to advise you on how to apply these tactics profitably. If you don't feel comfortable offering a discount, then don't. Not every industry is well-suited for daily deals.

**TRY THIS**:

Write down your ideas on what types of things you might offer for daily deals. Examples include: % or $ off, BOGO (buy one get one), incentives to bring a friend, incentives for repeat customers (e.g. get a free coffee on your third visit), gift cards, etc.

_____

_____

# NOTES

## INTERMEDIATE CHALLENGE:

List the strategies and tactics for participating in check-in sites (e.g. spending time signing up for and figuring out how to get your business to participate in Foursquare, hiring a professional to design a campaign for Facebook check-in, or meeting with your marketing team to decide on a clever offer/discount).

_____

_____

_____

_____

# NOTES

# BLOGS AND VLOGS

A blog is short for a "weblog," which is a log or journal on the web. Some blogs are more journal-like, yet others are professional with articles of journalistic quality. A blog can be one page with journal entries starting from most recent and going back in time, or it can be a full-blown website with lots of resources and other pages that have static information and evergreen articles ("evergreen," in this context means that the information is timeless).

Some people make pretty good money with their blogs (enough to pay their mortgage or take vacations). They do this by monetizing the blog when they have thousands or tens of thousands of followers. Monetizing means you sell something or have ads on the blog from which you make money.

The blog can either be a part of your website or it can be its own entity. You can even use a blog as the hub of your online presence in lieu of a website, depending on your business.

A vlog is a video log ("v" for video plus "log"). While you can post videos on your blog, if your entire thrust is video and you have very little text or articles, then what you have is a vlog.

Blogs and vlogs can help you with the following:

- Higher ranking for search engine results
- Increasing customer trust
- Establishing you as a thought leader or expert
- Brand awareness
- Educating prospects and customers
- Monetization of your knowledge

## FREQUENCY OF POSTING BLOG ARTICLES AND VLOG VIDEOS

Consistency is the key to successful blogging. If you decide to post one article a month, then be consistent and don't allow six weeks to pass before posting something. But what is the ideal frequency?

The more often you post, the better it is for SEO (search engine optimization). The search engines recognize that you are relevant and fresh when you post content frequently. One article a day is ideal, but not realistic for most business owners.

Try scheduling one article a week into your editorial calendar (for more information about creating an editorial calendar, see the **Content** chapter in Section III of this Playbook). If this is too daunting for you, then schedule two articles a month.

# NOTES

Tips for how to achieve ideal frequency (one article a week or two articles a month):

- Invite a guest blogger from a related industry to write an article.
- Go to www.fiverr.com and pay $5 for an article with good keywords in it that has something to do with your business or industry. This will be generic content, so do not use this option very often.
- Write more than one article at a time, and save the other articles for future postings.
- Curate content from other blogs but do not plagiarize. Write summaries and commentaries instead.

## LENGTH OF ARTICLES AND VIDEOS

According to conventional wisdom of content creation for the Internet, the ideal length of an article should be 300 – 600 words. See more information about this in Chapter 8: **Content**. If the article is longer than 800 words, you should definitely break it up into two distinct articles.

Videos should be very short, as well, due to attention span. For a vlog, videos should be under 5 minutes with few exceptions (e.g. conducting an interesting interview). It's okay to have videos as short at 30 seconds, if you can make the message impactful.

## TYPES OF ARTICLES AND VIDEOS

What should you write about? There is an entire chapter about **Content** (See Section III: Strategy and Content) in this Playbook.

Things to remember when it comes to content for your blog versus content on your website: the blog is for *fresh* content. Remember to post original content not generic industry articles, and never plagiarize or recopy in full others' articles. Even when you credit the author, it is bad form and illegal to repost another article in full: just write a synopsis paragraph and then provide a link to the article.

See exercises and challenges in the chapter on **Content** for the following: developing an editorial calendar (keeps you accountable and gives you ideas when you are stuck on what to write), tips on how to develop your own unique voice, and types of articles or videos you can create.

## LEVERAGING YOUR BLOG ARTICLE OR VLOG VIDEO

Now that you have created great content – an article or a video – be sure to announce it on other platforms that you are using: Facebook, LinkedIn, Twitter, and, of course, your website.

Announcing your content and promoting it on other platforms is called leveraging your content. This is an important part to blogging, and should be scheduled in your editorial calendar

# <u>NOTES</u>

as part of the process of creating the content. In other words, you write the article or create the video, then you post the content, then you promote the content – all in one sitting.

## TRY THIS:

Remember the importance of listening? Refer back to **Listening and Humility** (Section I, Chapter 4).

Set aside half an hour to read others' blogs. You can look at other businesses in your industry, or you can search for topics that are of personal interest.

Look for three things.

1.  Notice their topics: are they general articles about the industry or are the articles specific to their business?
2.  Notice their frequency of posting: are they posting every week, once a month, or less frequently?
3.  Notice the number of followers or subscribers (if this is posted).

Write down the date and time that you commit to a 30-minute exploratory session reading others' blogs. Or, do it right now.

Date: _____     Time: _____

Make notes, here, on ideas that you have for your blog and elements you may want to add:

_____

_____

_____

_____

## INTERMEDIATE CHALLENGE:

What is the purpose of the blog? Are you using it to educate your customers on advanced features and benefits of what you are selling? Are you promoting events? Gathering information from your customers? Facilitating communication between your company and your customers? Be specific on the purpose of the blog so that you can create your content accordingly.

# NOTES

Write down the purpose of your blog:

_____

_____

_____

_____

# NOTES

# EVENT PROMOTION AND MEETUP SITES

Websites where you can create and list your events are rising in popularity as a grassroots way to get the word out about your local event to specialized, niche demographics.

These websites are awesome for event promotion because of the hyper-local demographics. Event promotion and meetup websites also have professional event marketing tools such as customizable email invitations, ability to embed promotional videos in your listing, order processing services for your ticketed events, and more.

Eventbrite, Plancast, and Meetup are three great websites to get the word out about your events. FindGravy.com is also a good place to submit your event for promotion.

These websites can help you with the following:
- Promoting your events
- Geographically local exposure
- Credibility
- Higher ranking in search engine results
- Industry visibility
- Building community

While many events are free or purely social (especially with Plancast and Meetup.com), it's okay for businesses to list free events, events that are blatantly promotional, or charge for an event. Free events are a good idea as a "loss leader:" get qualified prospects to attend so that you can collect their contact information or sell them something at or after the event.

## MEETUP.COM

As of October 2013, Meetup.com has over 15 million monthly users with almost 3 million monthly RSVPs. The purpose of Meetup.com is to facilitate people to meet in person. Here is Meetup's concise mission statement:

> *"**Meetup's mission** is to revitalize local community and help people around the world self-organize. Meetup believes that people can change their personal world, or the whole world, by organizing themselves into groups that are powerful enough to make a difference."* (http://www.meetup.com/about/ accessed October, 2013)

# NOTES

It does cost money to set up a Meetup.com group of your own, but the cost is minimal: $12/month (as of October 2013). You can either set up a group for your company events and include other industry events, or you can join other existing groups for free.

You can create up to three groups per account on Meetup.com, so plan your groups with great focus and purpose. Do you want to bring in other industry experts to give informative talks? Would you like to host parties or other fun events? Do you want to facilitate networking groups to meet at your place of business?

Meetup.com's purpose is to help you get together *in person*. So, if you start a group with the intent of promoting webinars, your group may not get approved.

If you are charging a fee for your event or meeting, you can take payments through Meetup.com (they charge a small percentage), which is convenient and can help guarantee better attendance.

## PLANCAST.COM

Plancast is especially popular with iPhone users. Like Meetup, Plancast makes it easy to share the events on social media sites like Facebook and Twitter, once you list your event on their site.

One drawback to Plancast is that they do not facilitate collecting money for an event if you are charging a fee to attend. However, you can link to the webpage that your event is listed on for more information or to sign up and pay.

Plancast is sometimes called a "social calendar," and is somewhat similar to FourSquare in that friends announce their plans and their whereabouts for others to see and join in.

## EVENTBRITE.COM

Eventbrite has sold over 143 million tickets (some tickets are free, others are through PayPal or a credit card) as of October 2013.

Like Meetup.com, you can collect money for your event on Eventbrite through PayPal after they take a small percentage of the cost of the ticket.

Of the three sites (Meetup, Plancast, and Eventbrite), Eventbrite has the most comprehensive invitation management tools. You can send customized invitations to your email list, monitor how many were opened, and see how many clicked on the link to look at the event posting.

# **<u>NOTES</u>**

<u>Examples of Events</u>

Here are some examples of businesses and industries that you might not think normally hold "events," and some creative ways they target niche demographics:

1.  A local chiropractor holds a free monthly class on "Introduction to Functional Medicine." She starts her own Meetup group, but also lists on Eventbrite as a free event to get people into her office and meet her in person. She contacts other meetup groups that are interested in and organized around nutrition, lifestyle management, and natural medicine to offer giving the class to their members.

2.  A floral shop holds two free classes: "Flower Arranging" and "Choosing the Right Flowers: Traditional Meanings and Significance of Flower Species." The florist targets singles Meetup groups, horticulture groups, and other specific demographics. The strategy is to get the prospects into the flower shop, hoping they stay after the class to buy flowers and gifts.

3.  A financial advisor holds monthly workshops with various timely themes for a small fee, helping prospects get a handle on their finances. The angle is to obtain customers after trust is gained, in specific niche demographics to which the Financial Advisor markets.

Refer to the **Demographics** exercise you did earlier in this Playbook (Section I: Chaper 4) for ideas on search terms for Meetup groups.

These websites are a platform upon which to get the word out about your events. If you are not holding an Open House, educational classes, motivational seminars, sales events, introductory sessions, or other events, then this might be something you should consider!

Check list of event promotion websites and tools that you can use:
\_\_\_ Facebook
\_\_\_ Meetup
\_\_\_ Eventbrite
\_\_\_ Plancast
\_\_\_ FindGravy.com
\_\_\_ Evite or Mailchimp (invitations)
\_\_\_ Hootsuite
\_\_\_ Twitter
\_\_\_ LinkedIn
\_\_\_ Website

# <u>NOTES</u>

___ Blog

___ YouTube (trailers, videos)

___ YouTube (footage of the event)

___ Google+ events

Refer to the last page in Appendix B to find a master **tear-out sheet** that you can photocopy for tracking your event promotion activities. Use this checklist each time you hold an event, or participate in a conference or expo.

Don't dismiss the importance of social gatherings and goodwill. People love to socialize and participate in charitable events. Remember the tenets of good public relations: creating goodwill, recognition and a sense of brand awareness!

## TRY THIS:

Spend 20 minutes on looking at Meetup.com to discover what groups are active in your area. Use search terms from your demographics list, brainstorming what groups might be interested in your event.

Write down the date and time you will do this, or do it right now.

Date: _____     Time: _____

Notes on search terms used:

_____

_____

_____

_____

## INTERMEDIATE CHALLENGES:

1. Decide who is in charge of planning events for your business. Have a meeting with that person and plan out an event calendar for the entire year. Who will update the event announcements on Eventbrite, Meetup.com, and Facebook? Where else will you announce the event? Will you integrate your traditional marketing efforts with your Internet marketing efforts to promote the event(s)?

# <u>NOTES</u>

Write here notes about event planning and delegation:

_____

_____

_____

_____

2. Plan to take pictures and videos at the event. Write down, here, where you will post the pictures and videos. Who will be in charge of uploading them? Remember to write descriptions with good keywords when posting.

_____

_____

_____

_____

## ADVERTISING AN OFFER

Meetup.com also gives you the chance to be a "sponsor" for different groups. As of October 2013, it's free for businesses. All you have to do is sign up, create your offer and choose which groups you want to be a sponsor for. Being a sponsor does not mean you pay for the group. It simply means that you are giving a special deal that is only available for the members of the groups you sponsor. You can also offer a perk (a discount or special offer).

Since it is free to advertise, and since you are targeting very small numbers (typically groups range from 10 to a couple of hundred members), you should make the offer appealing. Take advantage of this free method of hyper-targeting your demographics!

## INTERMEDIATE CHALLENGE:

Spend 60-90 minutes on Meetup.com contacting organizers of groups that fit your demographics. Do not send a generic email that you copy and paste. Spend the extra effort and tailor your message to that organizer and that group and explain why you are a good fit. Make the offer appealing and special.

Organizers are found on the left hand side of the screen on each group's home page.

Do your homework first, by looking just below the organizers to view the sponsors and perks already being offered for that group. Resist the urge to offer a perk by clicking on the "offer a perk"

# NOTES

button. It is better etiquette to contact the organizers first by emailing them or going to a meetup and meeting them in person. This is especially true if you are not a member of the group.

Write down which groups you have contacted, and record your responses.

| Meetup group name | Date contacted | Response |
| --- | --- | --- |
| | | |
| | | |
| | | |
| | | |
| | | |
| | | |
| | | |
| | | |
| | | |

# NOTES

# ONLINE DIRECTORIES AND REVIEWS

Anniversary date of ubl.org: _____
(Date you signed up. You need to renew every year.)


ubl.org package: _____
(Premium recommended)


Ubl.org email address/login: _____
ubl.org password: _____


RelyLocal email: _____
RelyLocal password: _____


## ONLINE DIRECTORIES

So now your website is live! The problem is, unless you are listed with the major online directories, it might still be difficult for customers and prospects to find your website. Think of online directories as the equivalent of the Yellow Pages books. It's the same concept, only online directories are more critical than a listing in the Yellow Pages used to be because of how everything is interconnected (backlinks, cross-promotions, etc.) online.


These websites can help you with the following:
- Reputation management
- Customer loyalty
- Higher ranking in search engine results
- Customer trust


This is important. If you are a brick and mortar business (you have a physical office or retail space and not a post office box or home office), you need to sign up with **Universal Business Listing** (ubl.org) so that Internet users can find you.

Universal Business Listing (ubl.org) syndicates your profile listing to all of the major and most of the minor online directories. "Syndicates," in this context, means that you create your profile just once, and ubl.org publishes it on hundreds of online directories for you at the same time.

# NOTES

Ubl.org is the new Yellow Pages (and yes, you are still listed in the online version of Yellow Pages), but it's much less expensive and much more effective. It's like the Yellow Pages on steroids! Your bang for your buck is terrific because your website information is greatly increased in the Google rankings so that customers and prospects can find you more easily.

Go onto ubl.org and sign up for the Premium package to list your business. This is critical to help your website ranking in the search engines, as well as getting your website found by Internet users that stumble on your information via the online directories. Write in the information above (date signed up, etc.)

As there is a cycle for directory updating, you will have to wait for several months for the directories to list your business. So be patient.

## TRY THIS:

If you have a brick and mortar business, it's mandatory that you sign up for ubl.org. This is better than Yext, and more comprehensive and critical to your website successfully being found.

Sign up for the Premium package. Designate a minimum of 90 minutes to do this properly. Write down the date and time you will do this, or do it right now.

Date: _____          Time: _____

Use this checklist below for signing up:
_____ Photos of business or business owner
_____ Description with best keywords. Use up the maximum allowed space they give you to squeeze as many keywords and key phrases as possible.

## INTERMEDIATE CHALLENGES:

Some industries have more specialized directories that drill down a business category as distinguished from the more general directories such as Google Places or Yahoo Local. These specialized directories can be either hyper-local like St. Paul Clicker and BetterBuyQuick (these are examples in the Twin Cities in Minnesota), or they can be hyper-industry specific like Yoga Finder. Depending on the search terms that prospects and customers use, these specialized directories can rank higher in search results over the general directories.

Just a few examples of industry-specific directories include: chiropractors, yoga, financial services, veterinarians, funeral services. Ubl.org lists which professional groups it will additionally list you in, so check the website to see if you are in one of those industries: https://www.ubl.org/Products/ProfessionalGroups.aspx.

# <u>NOTES</u>

If your industry is not on this list, you should do a search for your "industry keywords AND location" (e.g. yoga AND Minneapolis) to see if specialized directories rank high.

1. Do an online search online for "your industry" AND "your city."
You will need about 20 minutes for this. Write down the date and time you will do this, or do it right now.

Date: _____          Time: _____

2. Use the space below to keep track of specialized directories (especially ones that are hyper-local) that you contact directly. Check back to make sure they have listed you correctly.

Some offer free listings in hopes that you upgrade to a paid membership in exchange for a prominent or featured listing. Only pay for one if it is in your budget, or if you think that you will get a high return directly from it. For example, many psychologists firmly believe that paying to be listed in Psychology Today is well worth it.

| Name of directory | Date contacted | Date listed |
|---|---|---|
| _____ | _____ | _____ |
| _____ | _____ | _____ |
| _____ | _____ | _____ |
| _____ | _____ | _____ |
| _____ | _____ | _____ |
| _____ | _____ | _____ |
| _____ | _____ | _____ |

# <u>NOTES</u>

_____    _____    _____

_____    _____    _____

_____    _____    _____

3. RelyLocal is a website that serves both as a directory and as a resource to help you promote your business online. Because of RelyLocal's critical mass with small, local business owners, you have an SEO (search engine optimization) advantage that helps customers find you.

While there is a small investment for participating in RelyLocal, this is an effective way to reach the conscious consumer demographic: buyers who want to spend their money on mom-and-pop businesses instead of larger corporations and chain stores.

Find out if there is an active RelyLocal business online for businesses in your city. Contact the owner by phone or email and have a discussion about how it can help you.

Date contacted: _____     Date of phone conversation or meeting: _____
Name of Rely Local owner or representative: _____

Notes:

_____

_____

_____

_____

## CUSTOMER REVIEW WEBSITES

Yelp username: _____
Yelp password: _____

Buyers have more confidence in peer reviews than they do in advertisements. You can say that you are the best dentist in the entire town, but if a dozen happy customers say it in their own words, it's more believable.

Remember, this is pull versus push marketing. You don't push your message out, shouting

# NOTES

from the rooftops: "Hey, look at me, I'm great! My pizza is great!" You let the happy customers shout from the rooftops: "Pretty good pizza, but it's the customer service that you gotta come in and experience!" or "...great place for kids and teens! And the pizza is awesome, too!"

Let them say it. Let the customers express their satisfaction. They are leaving reviews about your business online whether you know about it or not.

But what about bad reviews? You've heard the old advertising adage: "even bad press is still press." Well, the same holds true to some extent on the Internet. The trick is to manage the bad press, address it publicly and stay on top of communicating with unhappy customers.

The point is, don't be afraid of negative customer reviews. They are doing it regardless of whether you are actively participating in social media or not. When you engage these customers by addressing their concerns, it will mitigate the damage. This is called reputation management.

Review websites include Insider Pages, Google Maps, Bing Local, Yelp, Local.com, Yahoo Local, City Search, Merchant Circle. Reviews are also written on daily deals and check-in sites such as FourSquare (see section below, Daily Deals & Check-ins).

### TRY THIS:

1. Perform an online search of reviews for your business using the keywords "business name" AND "reviews."

Spend 10-15 minutes on this activity, allowing time to carefully read any reviews posted by users. Write down the date and time you will do this, or do it right now.


Date: _____        Time: _____


Notice the following as you are reading reviews:
- Review website (e.g. Google Places, Yelp)
- Username of reviewer
- Date of the review
- Comments or responses to the review


2. Go to Yelp.com, do the following, and put a check mark once completed:
_____ Sign up if you are not already by giving them your email and creating a password.
_____ See if there are already reviews about your business by doing a search in Yelp.
_____ Search your competitors and read reviews about their businesses.
_____ Write a review about a restaurant or car wash that you have patronized lately.

# NOTES

Yelp has a formula for deciding if you are a "legitimate" member of its community. If you only post one or two reviews, but do nothing for a long time, then Yelp sometimes will filter your review. It hides your reviews and does not count them towards the star rating if it doesn't think you are an active member. Keep this in mind when asking your happy customers to post reviews for you.

## INTERMEDIATE CHALLENGE:

Encourage your existing happy customers to list reviews online. It is more effective if they are already users of Yelp or Google Places reviews. If not, they can at least email you a testimonial that you can post on your website.

Here are some examples of tactics you can use to encourage customers to post reviews:

- Have a laptop at the front desk or cash register counter and let the customer log in to Yelp right while they are standing there.
- Make a poster to encourage and thank those who review your business and placing it near the exit of the business.
- Have conversations with your customers and simply ask them to post a review online
- Ask customers to post a review on their phone and post the review right now.

Highlight an idea that appeals to you from the list above, or write below tactics you will use to encourage customers to write reviews about your business.

# NOTES

# CHAPTER 6
# TOOLS AND TACTICS

*A note about outsourcing...*

Just as you would not put on a major PR event without hiring professionals to help make the event a success, you will want to seek out professional help to maximize your online marketing activities. This is especially true when it comes to utilizing tools and tactics.

## WHAT ARE TOOLS AND TACTICS?

Tools are things you use. Tools are important in the online marketing arena because they make all your efforts more effective and profitable. You will need to decide whether you want to learn how to wield some of these tools yourself or hire experts to really give your social media activities and online marketing a powerful "oomph."

Remember, one tool is never the one and only answer (to a hammer, everything looks like a nail). For example, email campaigns alone are not the only answer. You'll want sophisticated opt-in offers, well-designed graphics and well-written ad copy in addition to excellent SEO so that everything works in synergy.

Tools make your job easier. Tactics, on the other hand, are things you do. You employ tactics using tools to achieve your goals and objectives.

Remember, this is only an introductory Playbook to get you started in the fun game of social media and online marketing. Only jump in the tool box arena when you are ready. Call professionals and experts. Ask questions. Choose only what you feel comfortable with, what you understand and with what you resonate.

When spending money, refer to the budget in your **Online Marketing Plan**. See the chapter on **Strategy** (Section III: Chapter 1) for a template to use for creating your own plan. Budgeting helps you to justify your investment. Budgeting also helps you understand the bigger picture of

# NOTES

the plan so that you can see how the investment you are considering plays into the overall plan.

Here is a good list of advanced tools and tactics that you might consider using to increase the effectiveness of your social media marketing efforts.

# NOTES

# LIST OF TOOLS

Tools are things you use. Use tools to make your job easier and achieve better results.

## AUTOMATED TOOLS FOR POSTING CONTENT

HootSuite is an example of an automated tool for posting. While you still have to dictate and decide the content of your posts, you can automate it to some extent by blasting one post to several platforms (Twitter, Facebook, and LinkedIn) all at once.

All you have to do is sign up for free on Hootsuite, and you can send your posts all at once. Do this instead of logging on to each platform individually, and it will save you time. You can also plan your postings in advance and schedule them for later dates. For example, you can sit down on a Sunday night for two hours and schedule out your postings for the entire month for LinkedIn, Facebook and Twitter.

The ability to schedule your posts in advance does not preclude you from sending additional posts in between, as current events come up, and you have other ideas of what to share on your social media platforms.

## FACEBOOK APPLICATIONS

Enhancing your Facebook fan page is a good idea so that you can increase your number of fans, keep those fans engaged, and convert those fans into prospects and eventually buyers. Remember the social media mantra: "Turn loyal customers into raving fans. Turn raving fans into product evangelists." This applies, here.

Hire an experienced professional to help you with advanced applications and professional graphic design so that your branding is consistent and your activities are well-targeted. Quality graphic design is very important with Facebook, as users of this platform prefer visuals over text-based articles and information.

Applications include how to make custom tabs, sophisticated landing pages for selling an eBook or other offer, video applications, fan contests, professional cover photo design, etc. You can outsource some of this on www.fiverr.com for gigs starting at just $5.

## ANALYTICS

Analytics show tangible statistics of your social media activities and online marketing efforts. Analytics include specific measurables such as number of page views, conversion rates, where the traffic is coming from (links, keywords, ads, etc.), demographics of the traffic, and more.

# **NOTES**

If you do not know how to read analytics for each of the platforms you are using, it's best to hire a professional who can generate reports and help you interpret them so you can tweak your campaigns and activities to be more productive. Or, hire a tutor to show you once and get you set up.

Keep track of the following:
- Where are your visitors coming from?
- How many unique visitors are you getting per day?
- How are they finding you (from which links or using which keywords)?
- What page is getting the most traffic?
- Conversation rates

Importantly: track your conversion rates. "Conversion" refers to the rate of action (opt-in/lead generation, sales, etc.) given the overall number of visitors.

If you are tracking traffic you will be able to evaluate how to tweak your website for better performance and maximize your strengths, then note here what your plan is to track traffic in the future (e.g. take a class on website analytics, hire a professional to provide reports).

Remember, the website is only one component of having an online presence. The company website is only one platform upon which to convey your message. If you do not have other platforms and tools in place, it will be much harder for prospects and customers to find your business online.

Facebook and other platforms offer free analytics for the administrator. For example, you can see it for your Facebook page as soon as you log in. Which posts are more popular? Try and post more of those. Which posts get the most reach? Why do you think they got so much reach and can you replicate that?

## AFFILIATE PROGRAMS

Many people who only have a blog as their website but do not sell a product or service choose to "monetize" their blog by using affiliate programs. This entails putting another company's banner on your website and receiving a reward from that company each time someone clicks on it and buys something. For example, Amazon.com is a popular affiliate provider.

The reverse is true, as well, where you create an affiliate banner and ask others to put your banner advertisement on their website and you pay them for each click through or purchase.

Affiliate programs also increase your backlink exposure, increase website traffic, and also contribute to brand awareness. This is simply a tool to increase your exposure and your sales.

# NOTES

## WEBINARS, CLASSES, EBOOKS, AND DVDS

Classes, eBooks, and DVDs are good tools to better your chances of succeeding in your Internet marketing adventures.

Be judicious about which classes you take, as most are not free. Do you want to run a little harder and go a little deeper with Facebook? Then find a book, DVD or class that can help you with that. Do you want to get a better handle on SEO, then pursue that. Be strategic, though, about what you spend your time on. Remember, you can always outsource if it makes sense time and money-wise.

## SOPHISTICATED OPT-INS AND AD COPY

Opt-ins is a term used when you see an offer (usually free) but you must enter your email in order to receive the free offer. In other words, you "opt-in" to receive the offer.

Your opt-in offer is a tool to amass an email list of qualified prospects. Well-written ad copy and a worthwhile opt-in offer can generate a high quality email list that can then be used to further your agenda (gain clients, sell your product, etc.).

This is only a tool to build an email list of qualified leads. You turn qualified leads into warm prospects by following up with other marketing tactics.

# **NOTES**

# LIST OF TACTICS

Tactics are things that you do. Use tactics as part of your online marketing strategy to achieve your overall goals and objectives.

## SEARCH ENGINE OPTIMIZATION (SEO)

People search for an answer to a question or for entertainment using keywords. Great SEO will help them stumble on your business if your Internet presence is strategically maximized.

Most people think of keywords when they hear the term SEO. It's more than just keywords or key phrases. This tool also entails social bookmarking, appropriate backlinks, cross-promotion, leveraging of content and more.

According to Dan Zarrella, "…you probably don't need more SEO help. Most businesses would benefit much more from increasing content quantity and quality." (Zarrella, *The Science of Marketing*, 39- 40).

Search engines are smart. Write inherently good content, useful content, meaningful content, and you will be rewarded. This is called "organic SEO." Don't try and outsmart the search engines or buy your way to the top of the search engine rankings. Just be authentic and useful in your content.

## WEBINARS SWAPS

Webinar swaps involve a higher level of collaboration where those who conduct webinars agree to coordinate their exposure to each others' audiences. It's like joint advertising, only an online version.

Webinars are a great way to educate your audience of customers and prospects. Or, you can have training on how-to for what you sell, or you can give excellent and interesting information with the hopes of selling something at the end.

Host webinars as a tactic to draw more customers into your fold. Those that want the information you are providing become warm and hot leads for future sales.

## SOCIAL BOOKMARKING

What about Pinterest, you've been wondering? Pinterest is not a platform, per se. It is a site that facilitates what is called "social bookmarking."

Social bookmarking allows crowds to comment on and vote up or down specific pieces of content (articles, videos, pictures, etc.). This is a visual and tangible way to measure the virility (how viral, or how popular) an article, video, or picture has become.

# NOTES

## PINTEREST

Pinterest allows you to "pin" or "repin" pictures as if you are pinning something up onto a bulletin cork board, and comment on it if you want. This giant, virtual bulletin board also allows you to organize your pins into categories on "boards" (which is a way to group your pictures, like a filing system).

Pinterest is especially effective for businesses that lend well to visuals, videos, and pictures. Realtors, for example, have been using Pinterest to promote their listings. Use your graphics from your branding campaign to pin on Pinterest.

You can also use Pinterest to get customers and fans to participate in your brand. Run a contest requesting photo submissions, and leverage the contest by announcing it on other platforms, as well: Facebook, LinkedIn, Twitter, YouTube, and your website and/or blog. Look up Godiva and Maggiano's on Pinterest for examples on how to run a successful contest.

Other popular bookmarking sites (according to Alexa.com) include the following:
- Digg (where you can give a thumbs up or comment on an article)
- StumbleUpon (where you can flag content for others to stumble upon or vice versa)
- Reddit (a somewhat elite and competitive community)
- Delicious

Use this group of websites as a tactic to increase your reach and promote your content.

## EMAIL CAMPAIGNS

With a good email list, a coordinated marketing campaign (meaning, in this context, a specific purpose), and good value (meaning well-written content that provides value), you can conduct effective email campaigns to reach your target prospects. Again, this is a great way to reach very specific niche markets if conducted properly.

Hire a professional to help you design something that is effective and not a waste of time or money. Only do this is you have a sizeable email list and have something to offer.

Email campaigns are also a tactic to use to promote your social media links. Remember to add links to your primary platforms (e.g. Facebook, YouTube) to your business email signature.

# NOTES

166 | PLATFORMS AND TOOLS

# NOTES

## AD CAMPAIGNS

An ad campaign is where you pay for ads on either Google or Facebook (those are the primary two in the industry). Only do this if you can justify the returns in your budget. Some industries do very well by paying for Google AdWord campaigns.

The beauty of the ad campaigns online is that you can choose a daily budget or a per click budget. You can choose, say, $3/day or $.80/click. This is a great way to really control your budget and break it down to the ridiculous when figuring out your ROI.

## PPC/GOOGLE ADWORD CAMPAIGNS

Just like in traditional advertising, in the online world of advertising, you can pay to have your business more visible on other websites and in the search engines.

PPC stands for "pay per click" and is a type of advertising campaign used to generate traffic for your landing page with an offer, your online shopping cart, or your website. You pay for each Internet user that clicks on your ad. Hence, "pay per click."

PPC and Google AdWord campaigns may seem costly at first glance, but they are actually less expensive than traditional advertising, more tightly focused to specific demographics, and easily tailored to a specific, named budget.

## FACEBOOK AD CAMPAIGN

Facebook enables you to promote posts that you think will generate good leads or even sales (if you are selling something online). You can also promote events, a landing page, or an offer or discount.

What is great about the Facebook ad campaign is that you can choose your demographics carefully, down to age and gender, location, and more. This way, you expose your promotion only to those whom you want to see it that fall into niche demographics.

You have a choice on Facebook as to whether you want to pay by exposure or pay for clicks. This is a great way to control your budget if you choose to use this type of ad campaign.

## CONTENT LEVERAGING

Content, remember, is video, text, comments, or photo. Leveraging that content means that you announce across all online platforms that you have posted it!

For example, if you create a video and upload it onto your YouTube channel but don't announce it to anyone, then you are not leveraging that content across your social media platforms and audiences. Announce your video by linking to it on your Facebook page, embedding it into

# NOTES

your website, and tweeting about it. Post a link on your blog to the video, and share it with your connections on LinkedIn.

## PROFESSIONAL BRANDING

Yes, branding is still important, even in the digital age. Yes, advertising agencies and some webmasters can help with professional branding strategies and brand awareness campaigns. It's never too early to brand yourself.

Go back to the beginning of this Playbook and review the section about Mission Statements. Incorporate your mission and your values into your brand. That is how you are distinct from others in your industry.

Branding is a tactic to make your business stand out among the competition. Branding is more than just company reputation or snazzy, professional graphics and images. Branding is a unique identity and should help you with your positioning in the marketplace.

## PHONE APPLICATIONS

You've heard the mantra: "There's an app. for that!" Well, if there isn't, then did you know that you can create one? For a small investment, you can hire someone to create a phone app. for your company. Further, if you want to get really sophisticated, you can sell advertising to horizontal markets (related industries) to subsidize your phone app.

Mobile users exceed laptop and desktop computer users, now. More people access the Internet via a mobile device than they do from a traditional computer. Go to your customers. Don't expect them to come to you randomly. Meet them where *they* are.

## BLOG MONETIZATION

There are other ways to monetize your blog besides affiliate programs. Selling eBooks, webinars, and products on your blog are also viable options.

You can sign up for Amazon affiliates, or Google Adsense, or both. You can use affiliate banner ads, or you can sell something of your own making (eBook, DVD, or webinars).

## OFFERING A DVD OR EBOOK

Besides the obvious benefit of leaving a legacy, you can earn residual income by offering a DVD or eBook that you create. This is a good way to create another income stream to the mix of what you already have going on.

You create the book or DVD once, and then it sells in perpetuity. Even if the income is mea-

# NOTES

ger, the residual aspect of having something to sell that you created just once is a good idea.

In the context of Internet marketing, though, you can use this tactic as a way to increase your credibility, increase your reach and exposure, increase your email list of hot prospects (whoever buys your item will want more from you), and fill your sales funnel.

# SECTION III
# STRATEGY
# AND CONTENT

# NOTES

# CHAPTER 7

# STRATEGY

You cannot begin to create content (articles, videos, etc.) until you have a strategy. Yes, of course you want to write about your business. But remember the **Demographics** challenge (Section I: Chapter 4) that you completed at the beginning of the book? Refer back to that, again, so that we can begin to carefully craft a strategy.

Just as in speaking, in creating content, you have to keep the audience in mind. This is a mantra for all professional speakers. Incorporate this into your strategy. Who is your audience? What is your demographic target?

Purpose is also critical. Professional speakers know this, too: "What is the purpose of the speech (or content)?" Is the purpose to sell, to educate, to retain current customers? Or perhaps you want to entertain to inspire loyalty, encourage expression from your fans, or even to stir up controversy for a public relations stunt. There are many, many types of purposes for content. Be clear on what you are trying to achieve.

Remember, then: combine keeping the audience in mind with the purpose of the website or other platform, and you have a winning combination.

Now, let's create a formal Online Marketing Plan.

## YOUR ONLINE MARKETING PLAN

Congrats on working your way through the Playbook! Armed with the knowledge of which platforms will give you the biggest bang for your buck and that resonate with you and your company's mission, you are now ready to create your Online Marketing Plan.

Just as you began your business with a formal Business Plan and possibly an overall Marketing Plan, it's important that you don't just jump into the foray of social media or online marketing without a game plan.

# NOTES

We've all heard the mantra: "Businesses who fail don't plan to fail, they fail to plan."

Creating and using an Online Marketing Plan as a compass and a road map is the single smartest business decision you will make when it comes to being successful at engaging in social media. Plan on it!

Strategies, as distinguished from tactics, are an over-arching planning issue that supports goals.

Tools, remember, support your tactics. Here are a few examples:

1. Launching an email marketing campaign and creating and promoting a landing page for an e-book are two tactics employed to support the strategy of building an email list of qualified prospects. The objective is to feed the sales force with more leads so you can achieve your goal of increased sales.

2. SEO, content leveraging, and social bookmarking are tactics that can be used to help your strategy of getting your content to go viral. The goal is to increase reach and influence so that your branding is more effective. An automatic posting site like Hootsuite is a tool to help you with the tactic of leveraging content.

3. Selling an e-book or conducting webinars online are tactics that support the strategy of creating additional revenue streams. The goals are to diversify, create residual income, and leave a legacy. Createspace.com is a tool to help you with the tactic of publishing an e-book, while gotomeeting.com is a tool to help you with the tactic of conducting webinars.

Keep these distinctions in mind when planning. You don't want to be a strategy-less tactician running around implementing lots of Internet marketing tactics only to be disappointed that you are not getting results. Wars and games are won with effective use of the three-legged stool of tools, tactics and strategy. If you are missing a leg, the stool falls down.

## TRY THIS:

Create a formal marketing plan for your business. This can be a simple one page "Online Marketing Plan." Use the template below to craft your own strategy.

Type up a one-page summary of your over-arching Online Marketing Plan that includes the following components:

**Mission Statement.** You can use your current Mission Statement for your business, but it would be more effective to create an Online Marketing Mission Statement specifically designed to be a compass for your online and social media efforts.

**Values Statement.** Use the one that you already have in your business plan. If you don't have

# <u>NOTES</u>

one, then create one now. Your values are unique to you and should also serve as a compass when making individual decisions about online activities. Stick to your values.

**List of online platforms that you plan to use and WHY.** If you do not want to use daily deals, for example, because you feel that it is not appropriate for your business or industry or for your demographics, then do not include that. If you think that YouTube has a lot of potential for marketing campaigns, then describe some directions that the business might take with that and tie them to your values.

**Initial division of labor.** List your team and describe each person's role. For example: Mary Smith will be primarily in charge of Facebook and Twitter posts, the company owner will be in charge of creating profile information, and John Jones will be in charge of YouTube video campaigns. All of us will be responsible for increasing subscribers, etc.

Be courageous and anoint team members with clever, playful titles. For example, Mary Smith is the TweetMaster, and John Jones is the Video Guru. Blogmeister, Graphics Queen, and Facebook Whiz are more examples of fun titles you can assign your team members.

**Time budget.** The old saying "time is money" is true. Every minute you spend doing one thing means you are not doing another. You need to look at what you spend time on and prioritize. Spend more time on things that will get you closer to success, less on everything else. Make a time budget.

**Monetary budget.** Just as you budget your time, you need to budget your marketing money as well. Make a list of all marketing related expenditure in the last month, or last quarter. That is your baseline budget. Then analyze what you got for it. Eliminate the things that didn't work, and add new ones to try. That will be your new budget. Do a monthly, quarterly, and annual budget.

**Tools and resources.** Decide which tools will support your strategies and tactics. What will help you be successful?

Refer to the Appendix for a template you can fill in to create your Online Marketing Plan.

# NOTES

# CHAPTER 8
# CONTENT

"Content is King and SEO is Queen" is a common expression heard among social media professionals. What this means is that you must be found and heard online. Content is King because you must write quality articles that are relevant to the reader. But that great content must be found! It needs to be well-keyworded and promoted for the Queen to compliment your great information.

In the Internet marketing world, it's not true that if you build it, they will come. Readers and viewers will not come unless you announce your content. Announcing it is not enough, either. Your content has to be relevant and interesting. You need both the King and the Queen.

Always remember to keep the reader in mind. Keeping the audience in mind will help you write for them, not for yourself. Don't compose hard sell messages. Remember that online marketing is pull marketing.

Keeping the reader in mind means adhering to the etiquette and rules of each online community. Refer back to **The Big "Why" is the Sense of Community** (Section I: Chapter 1) to review how important communities are to your prospects and customers.

What types of content are there? Articles and videos are the most obvious. Tweets and Facebook posts count as content, as well. The text that you write for videos and pictures are also counted as content, proving valuable for keywords in search engines. Even what you write in your LinkedIn profile is content. Reviews are content, whether you write for other businesses or customers write them for you. And the description of an offer or deal or discount is considered content.

Posting a comment on another website or blog is content, as well!

# <u>NOTES</u>

## CONTENT: TEXT

The blog is where you will post most of your text content. While your website contains static text, a blog is where *fresh* content should be posted on a regular basis. Generic articles are not good use of a blog space. It's okay to curate content instead of creating your own, as long as the content is a) not copyrighted and b) interesting and useful. You can link to others' articles, but it's not good practice to repost articles in full, even if attributed.

Don't be afraid to hire a ghostwriter for quality articles. Useful information cultivates followers, and well-keyworded content adds to your SEO (search engine optimization) tactics. Content editors can be great resources, as well.

Search engines penalize for the following, so DON'T do these things:

1. Generic content.
2. Articles with "overstuffed" keywords and key phrases. Don't overdo it, just write naturally.
3. Reprinting articles in full (even if it is your own content) on multiple sites. Do not reprint your articles on multiple sites, even if you own them (the articles and the websites). Either rework the articles for a slightly different spin, or summarize and link to the original.

## TRY THIS:

Here, below, write a list of article title ideas that you will either write yourself, outsource to an editor or ghostwriter, or curate from others' websites (or a combination of all of those).

**ARTICLE IDEAS** (remember to edify, educate or entertain):

_____

_____

_____

_____

Develop a regular posting schedule of content, as this will improve the ranking of your website. Frequency is important because your readers begin to trust you and like you. Customers do business with those they like and trust.

Create an **editorial calendar** to help keep yourself accountable to frequency of writing and to help you when you might be stuck for ideas on what to write. Refer to the challenge below for ideas on how to create an editorial calendar for your Internet marketing content.

Work toward developing a unique voice, or tone. The blog can be both informative and playful in the sense that you can show your personality and your character. Ideas for blog content can

# NOTES

be culled from brainstorming sessions with your employees, customers, or a social media marketing coach. You can also investigate what others are writing about in their blogs.

## LENGTH OF ARTICLES

Here are some tips on article length:

- Articles should be a minimum of 250 words for Google to index it as an actual article and not a "blurb," and a maximum of 800 words in accordance with online reader attention span. If your article is over 800 words, then narrow the focus and break it into two articles.

- Ideal word range for articles = 300- 600 words.

- Learn how to compartmentalize the information so that you chunk articles into readable bits. If an article is too wordy, then break it in half! For example, you cannot cover the care of Begonias in one article. You might write a series of articles on Begonias: introduction to Begonias, water and sun, pruning, propagating, colors and varieties, getting the most of your blooms, etc. Similarly, you can write lots of little articles that are interesting and informative for you readers that have narrowly-defined topics.

Contact Coach Angela for ideas and help on what articles you can write for your blog or website. Coach.angela@yahoo.com

## ARTICLE WEBS

You can create an article web when you have achieved some critical mass in terms of number of articles or webpages you have written. You can create a "web" by hyperlinking them together within the body of the articles. If you use the example, above, of the Begonias, then you would interlink them all together to keep the reader on your blog or website.

Article webs are also a very good way to leverage your content. When you leverage your content, you get a better bang for your buck – or a better readership and reach for your efforts.

## CONTENT: VIDEOS

Videos rank over 50 times higher than text in search engines if properly keyworded and with great SEO (search engine optimization). You can learn how to do this yourself, hire a coach who can teach you how to do it yourself, or hire a professional to handle all your videos – from production to editing to keywording.

Resist the urge to be promotional. Avoid talking head videos where the owner of the company talks about how he or she is earnest in delivering great customer service. Videos should be interesting, and not blatant commercials. But what is interesting?

# <u>NOTES</u>

Here is a list of content that could be interesting, informative, or even entertaining:

- Interviews of popular or controversial people
- How-to videos
- Self-help videos
- Demonstrations
- Contests – user-submitted videos
- Humorous videos (when appropriate, inoffensive, and politically correct)
- Inspirational videos that are relevant to your business
- Scientific or technical lectures (appealing to the analytically-minded audiences)
- Testimonials from happy customers (avoid talking heads, try to add scenic interest or activities)

The key to video content, as with text content, is leveraging. You post it on YouTube and/or your website and/or your blog, you will want to promote the content by announcing it via Facebook, Twitter, LinkedIn and on your website. Announcing your interesting content via traditional print media is also a way to drive traffic to your website and platforms hosting your content (YouTube, blog or website). For example, a postcard mail campaign might contain a web address or QR code that drives customers and prospects to your YouTube channel or website.

## CONTENT: PICTURES

Post pictures on your website, blog, LinkedIn, and Facebook. Search engines consider pictures as content, so it is very important that you describe your pictures with good keywords when you post them.

Search engines sometimes will rank an article higher in search results simply because the picture's keywords match the search. This is a considering factor for SEO.

Also, rotating pictures is a good idea for several reasons:

1. Search engines think that you are posting fresh content. Fresh is good, as it is a factor in SEO and how you rank in search results.
2. Keep professional pictures of you current, or you will lose credibility when people meet you if you don't look the same. Profile pictures are critical in some industries where consumers want to know you are a trustworthy and "normal" person.
3. Show up in **Images** search results when you post multiple, well-keyworded pictures. Some people are searching for images, some people might search your name as an images search, and this will help with increasing your exposure.
4. Facebook users are very visual and love to see pictures.

# NOTES

Take pictures of your business like a proud parent takes pictures of their kids! Take pictures at events, or designate someone to do so, and post them on the Internet. Take pictures of your office, your customers (make sure they sign a release form allowing you to use the pictures), and any exciting achievements you want to show off to everyone.

## CONTENT: COMMENTS

It is a great idea to post comments on other people's blogs. Make sure your comments are encouraging and substantial to contribute to the discussion or add to the article. Comments give you more visibility, especially if you link to your website. Don't ever be blatantly promotional – that's not good etiquette.

The benefits of commenting are creating good backlinks to your website or YouTube channel, increasing credibility, increasing visibility, fostering relationships, and promoting goodwill in the online community.

Allowing comments on your blog is highly recommended. Remember, even "bad" press is press. If the comments are negative or argumentative, that is okay. Controversy drives more traffic to the blog or YouTube channel as comments can get lively and even heated at times. This is okay because the article or blog post could go viral!

## CONTENT: TWEETS

Tweets should contain the link one quarter of the way into the tweet instead of at the end. Also, use action words like verbs and adverbs. Don't say, "weight loss video (link) funny and interesting."

Here are good examples:

1. Click here to laugh (link) and then retweet to anyone wanting to #loseweight and eliminate #cellulite.
2. #loseinches, #laugh & watch this (link). Please rt if you think it's a #funnyvideo.
3. hilarious! #weightloss video (link). Retweet if it made you laugh.

These tweets have a call to action (laugh, retweet, watch). These tweets pique interest, as you want to know what is so funny.

## CONTENT: FACEBOOK

When it comes to Facebook, photo posts perform the best, according to Zarrella's *The Science of Marketing*. Have you seen photos with cynical, funny, or inspirational quotes imposed on them? Those are called "memes." A meme in this context is a unit (the picture with the quote) that carries

# <u>NOTES</u>

a cultural idea to replicate and mutate as it spreads. Memes can go viral very quickly.

Calls to action are effective posts. Ask for the "like" in your post. It's a call to action. Say, "click like if you know that chiropractic is beneficial for kids." Or, "click like if you are in favor of green construction."

All content must be organic and authentic. This is especially true for posts on Facebook. "Click like to welcome Amy as the newest member of our team." Or, "click like to congratulate us on winning this award." Or, "click like if you think we should run a holiday special on (product)."

"Facebook users seem to want more than short sound bite-style content. They want to read the story behind the stories they're hearing on the nightly news, not just the same things everyone else is saying." (Zarrella, *The Science of Marketing*, 99)

## CREATING AN EDITORIAL CALENDAR FOR YOUR CONTENT

An editorial calendar is a planning tool. Use a blank calendar and plug in times and dates of when you will create your content. You can brainstorm and put titles of articles or video ideas, then write them down in a time slot on certain dates.

Also sometimes called a Content Plan, there are several ways that you can plan your content ahead of time. Remember, this is all about strategy. We are not just randomly pushing out a message. Your content has to be consistent with your brand, and give value to your audience.

For example, you could dedicate every Monday afternoon from 2 p.m. to 3 p.m. to writing an article for your blog. Make a list of possible article titles, and fill in your calendar for every Monday for a month or two. You are not bound to write on that topic, but if you are stuck for a topic, you can just write on that.

A more sophisticated way to create your editorial calendar would be to plan themes or campaigns. For example, you could write about weight loss for six weeks in a row, pushing the theme in January when New Year's resolutions are at their peak. You could plan for posting articles and videos (say, three articles a month, and two videos a month that you create, and other articles that you curate to fill in between). Then, you could move other themes as appropriate to seasons, holidays, and trends.

The calendar will help you to carve out the time to do your social media, as well. You could schedule ten minutes a day, at a specific time of day, to post on Hootsuite or Facebook, for example.

The editorial calendar helps you to hold yourself accountable for posting content, but should also be helpful when you are stuck on what topics to write about. Plan far in advance in one sitting, and your life will be much easier when it comes to implementing.

# <u>NOTES</u>

**TRY THIS**:

Make an editorial calendar.

Create a recurring entry in your electronic calendar for a time that you commit to writing an article or posting on your social media sites for 60 or 90 minutes. Make it once a week, or once a month.

If you do not use an electronic calendar on your phone, in Microsoft Outlook, or on your computer, then use a paper calendar. Here are some options for paper calendars:

1. Buy a large desk top calendar from Office Depot.
2. Print free monthly calendars from www.printable2013calendars.com (or, www.printable-2014calendars.com).
3. Use your wall calendar.

Another option is to create a spreadsheet in Excel. The social media experts at www.webolutions.com can help you with planning your content on a spreadsheet, and give tips on how to use broadcasting tools such as HootSuite and TweetDeck.

Be specific when scheduling. Checklist for your editorial calendar:

☐ Post *specific* dates and time slots (e.g. 15 minutes)

☐ Schedule *specific* activities (do NOT schedule a "social media time" or general "time on the Internet"). Examples: Browse for blog articles, select YouTube videos appropriate to post on Facebook, write a blog article, spend 20 minutes on Facebook to post and connect with friends)

☐ Pencil in a *specific* topic or title of articles and videos.

☐ Remember to include time to promote what content you create.

# SECTION IV
# CONCLUSION

# <u>NOTES</u>

# CHAPTER 9
# CONCLUSION

# CONCLUSION AND PUTTING
# IT ALL TOGETHER

Be careful not to overload on your social activities too soon. For example, join a handful of groups on LinkedIn – only a choice few that you feel comfortable participating in and reading through. In other words, don't over-commit by joining too many groups or following too many people that you can't keep up.

Refer to your Online Marketing Plan and revise it when appropriate. Let it serve as a reminder of your overall goals of participating in online marketing and social media: interacting with prospects and customers to establish greater trust.

Use your editorial calendar to help you adjust your time commitment as needed. Be diligent in promoting your content across all platforms you are using at the same time you create and post your content. Do not procrastinate promotion of your content.

Remember to be genuine and not pushy or over-promotional. Let your personality shine through in your communications. This is SOCIAL media, not thinly-disguised advertising and blatant promotional commercials. Use common sense and courtesy when it comes to etiquette in communicating online. These are communities, and the sense of community is why you are participating.

Again, trust is gained when credibility is established. Credibility is established by increased visibility, consistency, expert comments and articles, and your genuine human personality shining through for all to see online.

It takes patience and persistence to build your online presence, just as it takes patience and

# NOTES

persistence to build relationships. Keep plugging away at it and soon you will see some momentum build even if your content never goes viral. Slow and steady wins the race.

Take the long view when it comes to online marketing. This means that you will not see explosive, tangible results immediately. Exercise patience and understand that it takes time to build momentum and critical mass when it comes to building an audience.

Always remember that there is no substitute for in-person relationship building, no shortcuts to marketing either via traditional means or via online outlets, and no shortcuts to being authentic with great customer service. Increasing your online presence and participating in social media are just tools- modern advertising and marketing tools.

Again, congrats for making the bold leap into the big, wide world of online marketing. Keep this Playbook as a resource and a record-keeping tool to keep track of your progress in the early stages of your journey.

Also, keep the Playbook handy so you can look up social media and online marketing terms in the glossary.

## PUTTING IT ALL TOGETHER

You've learned a lot during the course of this Playbook! Let's boil it down and recap so it becomes a simple matter of following these steps. Take these steps in order to put all the information together that you learned in this Internet Marketing Playbook:

## STEPS TO IMPLEMENT FOR INTERNET MARKETING

1.  Listen. Scope out the competition. Get a handle on your online reputation. Listen to the tone and understand the needs of online communities. Listen between the lines: is there something you can help with?

2.  Branding/niche. Tightly define your demographics. Explore every niche and be respectful that each community has needs and a unique identity. Brand according to your unique identity.

3.  Mission Statement. Announce your mission statement, and boldly revise it as necessary. This is inextricable from your branding and lends to your level of authenticity in the eyes of online communities.

4.  Platforms & Strategy. Now that you understand not just what the platforms are, but what they can do for you, **just choose two or three to work with initially.** Build your strategy around focusing tightly on just those platforms and do not get distracted. Use the template in the Appendix to create your Online Marketing Plan.

# <u>NOTES</u>

5. Create content. You are only ready to create content when you have identified which platforms you are going to concentrate on and when you have developed your strategy. See how there is a natural progression of doing these steps to increase your online presence? Be consistent with your content. Remember, slow and steady wins the race.

6. Implementation & Tactics. Post your content, implement your tactics, and be consistent. Follow your editorial calendar to help you keep yourself accountable.

7. Analyze & Tweak Strategy. Look at analytics available to you, tweak your strategy accordingly. What is working? What is not working? Do you need to boost your activities or try another strategy?

8. Repeat steps 1 through 7. Consistency and persistence wins the race. You will not get 1,000 followers and instant fame in a matter of a week or month. Keep applying the principles, and you will be successful.

Eat this elephant (online marketing) one bite at a time. Just get your arms around the big picture, pick two or three platforms to concentrate on, and finally go forth and implement.

Good luck with your new adventure!

# APPENDICES

# NOTES

# ONLINE PRESENCE ASSESSMENT

by Coach Angela, LLC

Initial Assessment Date: _____

Follow-up Assessment Date: _____

Name and Position: _____

Name of Business: _____

Industry: _____

Website Address: _____

## DEMOGRAPHICS

1. Do you know what social media platforms (e.g. Facebook, Twitter) your prospects and customers are using?                    Yes___          No___

If yes, briefly describe: _____

_____

_____

_____

2. Please describe the demographics of your customers as best you can (e.g. geography, age, income range, other): _____

_____

_____

_____

## CURRENT ONLINE ACTIVITY: GENERAL

1. Do you have a website?                          Yes ___          No ___
2. Is there a mobile version of your website?      Yes ___          No ___
3. Do you have help with ongoing online activity (e.g. posting comments, content creation, etc.)?                          Yes ___          No___

If yes, please describe (names, functions, etc.)

_____

_____

_____

4. List analytics you are using to track online activity: _____

_____

_____

5. Do you have a shopping cart online?          Yes ___          Not yet ___     n/a ___

6. Does your website have good SEO (search engine optimization)? Yes ___ No ___

If no, what is your strategy for improving the SEO? (e.g. hire a webmaster or SEO

expert)? _____

_____

## CURRENT ACTIVITY: PLATFORMS

1. Do you have a Facebook page?          Yes___          Not yet ___

   a.  Is it a Fan page or a Profile? _____

   b.  Do you have a call to action on your landing page?     Yes ___          No ___

   c.  # of fans who have "liked" your business page? _____

   d.  Frequency of posts? 1/day_____ 1/week_____ other: _____

   e.  Types of posts (check all that apply)

      ____ article links

      ____ videos

      ____ announcements

      ____ events

      ____ humor

      ____ educational tidbits

      ____ links to websites

      ____ pictures

      ____ videos

      ____ promotions

2. Do you have a YouTube Channel?          Yes_____          Not yet_____

   a. # of videos uploaded: _____

   b. # of subscribers: _____

   c. # of views for most popular video: _____

d. Do you have a regular schedule of uploading videos?   Yes _____ No _____

e. Do the videos double up as content for your website, as well? Yes _____ No _____

3. Do you have a blog?      Yes_____      No_____

    a. Name of blog: _____

    b. Address of blog: _____

    c. # of followers: _____

    d. Is your blog monetized? Yes _____ No _____

4. Do you have a LinkedIn profile?      Yes_____ No_____

    a. What percent is the profile filled out? _____%

    b. # of groups you belong to? _____

    c. # of connections: _____

    d. # of recommendations: ____

5. Do you have pictures of yourself and of your business that are appropriate for online profiles?      Yes___      No___

6. Do you use Twitter?      Yes_____      No_____

      a. # of followers: _____

      b. # you are following: _____

7. Listings in online directories:

a. Are you a subscriber to Universal Business Listing?  Yes_____      No_____

b. If no, in which online directories are you listed:

    _____ Bing

    _____ Google Places

    _____ Yahoo Local

    _____ Yelp (# of reviews: ___)

    _____ Angie's List

    _____ Foursquare

    _____ Yellowbot

    _____ City Search

    _____ Merchant Circle

    Other: _____

8. Daily Deals:

      a. Are coupons appropriate for your business?  Yes ___      No ___

      b. Have you ever offered online coupons?      Yes ___      No ___

If yes, please describe (venue, success rate, etc.) _____

_____

_____

9. Local Meetup and Event listing sites:
    a. Do you host events?                 Yes ____      No ____
    b. If so, what type of events? (e.g. classes, how-to workshops, Open House, semi-nars, awards galas, Public Relations stunts) _____

            _____

    c. Where do you list events? (check all that apply)
        ____ Eventbrite
        ____ Evite
        ____ Meetup.com
        ____ Plancast
        ____ Facebook
        ____ Other _____
10. Do you have a Google+ business page set up? Yes ____    No ____

## BUDGET
1. What is your weekly time budget for online activity? _____hour(s)/week
2. What is your monthly financial budget for online marketing? $_____/month
3. What is your monthly print budget for advertising? $_____/month

Name specific benefits that you wish to obtain from participating in online marketing:

_____

_____

_____

_____

# ONLINE MARKETING PLAN
### by Coach Angela, LLC

*Use this template, below, to create your own Online Marketing Strategic Plan.*

**Mission Statement.** You can use your current Mission Statement for your business, but it would be more effective to create an Online Marketing Mission Statement specifically designed to be a compass for your online and social media efforts.

_____

_____

_____

_____

_____

_____

**Values Statement.** Use the one that you already have in your business plan. If you don't have one, then create one now. Your values are unique to you and should also serve as a compass when making individual decisions about online activities. Stick to your values.

_____

_____

_____

_____

_____

_____

**List of online platforms that you plan to use and WHY.** If you do not want to use daily deals, for example, because you feel that it is not appropriate for your business or industry or for your demographics, then do not include that. If you think that YouTube has a lot of potential for marketing campaigns, then describe some directions that the business might take with that and tie them into your values.

_____

_____

_____

_____

_____

_____

**Initial division of labor.** List your team and describe each person's role. For example: Mary Smith will be primarily in charge of Facebook and Twitter posts, the company owner will be in charge of creating profile information, and John Jones will be in charge of YouTube video campaigns. All of us will be responsible for increasing subscribers, etc.

_____

_____

_____

_____

_____

_____

Be courageous and anoint team members with clever, playful titles. For example, Mary Smith is the TweetMaster, and John Jones is the Video Guru. Blogmeister, Graphics Queen, and Facebook Whiz are more examples of fun titles you can assign your team members.

_____

_____

_____

_____

_____

_____

**Time budget.** The old saying "time is money," well it is true. Every minute you spend doing one thing means you are not doing another. You need to look at what you spend time on and prioritize. Spend more time on things that will get you closer to success, less on everything else. Make a time budget.

_____

_____

_____

_____

_____

_____

**Monetary budget.** Just as you budget your time, you need to budget your marketing money as well. Make a list of all marketing related expenditure in the last month, or last quarter. That is your baseline budget. Then analyze what you got for it. Eliminate the things that didn't work, and add news one to try. That will be your new budget. Do a monthly, quarterly, and annual budget.

_____

_____

_____

_____

_____

_____

**Tools and resources.** Decide which tools will support your strategies and tactics. What will help you be successful?

_____

_____

_____

_____

_____

# NOTES

# APPENDIX B: MASTER PASSWORD LIST

Keep this password list with the Playbook, or you can photocopy or tear out this page and keep in a safe place.

## ONLINE PASSWORD MASTER LIST

### Website
URL: _____

Domain host name: _____

Domain password: _____

Web designer/programmer's name: _____

Web designer/Programmer's e-mail & phone: _____

### Blog
URL: _____

Domain host name: _____

Domain password: _____

Domain host e-mail & phone: _____

Webmaster/administrator password: _____

### Facebook
Email: _____

Password: _____

### YouTube
Email: _____

Password: _____

### Twitter
Username: _____

Password: _____

# ONLINE PASSWORD MASTER LIST (CONT'D)

## LinkedIn

Email: _____

Password: _____

## Ubl.org

Email: _____

Password: _____

## Meetup.com

Email: _____

Password: _____

Co-Organizers: _____

## HootSuite

Email: _____

Password: _____

## Yelp

Email: _____

Password: _____

## Merchant Circle

Email: _____

Password: _____

## Manta.com

Email: _____

Password: _____

## Eventbrite

Email: _____

Password: _____

# ONLINE PASSWORD MASTER LIST (CONT'D)

### FourSquare
Username: _____

Password: _____


### Google+
Username: _____

Password: _____


### Paypal
Username: _____

Password: _____


*Add your own platforms and keep track of them here.*

_____
### Name of platform
Username: _____

Password: _____


_____
### Name of platform
Username: _____

Password: _____


_____
### Name of platform
Username: _____

Password: _____


_____
### Name of platform
Username: _____

Password: _____

# NOTES

# APPENDIX C: TRACKING SHEETS
# FOR PLATFORM ACTIVITY

Feel free to tear out the Master Password list to keep it separate from the Playbook if you wish. Also, feel free to photocopy the tracking sheets if they work well for you.

Passwords can either be kept in the Playbook in each platform section, or in the following tear-out sheet to be kept separately.

Don't be afraid to create your own tracking sheets if other metrics are important to you, or if you evolve into more sophisticated analytics. For example, you might start tracking your conversion rates, etc.

The Event Promotion tracking sheet is a Master copy. Please photocopy before using it! This way, you can use the sheet for all your events, no matter how frequent or infrequent. This is a great checklist for websites on which you can promote your events.

# FACEBOOK FANS TRACKING SHEET

Date/# of fans: _____     Date/# of fans: _____     Date/# of fans: _____

Date/# of fans: _____     Date/# of fans: _____     Date/# of fans: _____

Date/# of fans: _____     Date/# of fans: _____     Date/# of fans: _____

Date/# of fans: _____     Date/# of fans: _____     Date/# of fans: _____

Date/# of fans: _____     Date/# of fans: _____     Date/# of fans: _____

Date/# of fans: _____     Date/# of fans: _____     Date/# of fans: _____

Date/# of fans: _____     Date/# of fans: _____     Date/# of fans: _____

Date/# of fans: _____     Date/# of fans: _____     Date/# of fans: _____

Date/# of fans: _____     Date/# of fans: _____     Date/# of fans: _____

Date/# of fans: _____     Date/# of fans: _____     Date/# of fans: _____

Date/# of fans: _____     Date/# of fans: _____     Date/# of fans: _____

Date/# of fans: _____     Date/# of fans: _____     Date/# of fans: _____

Date/# of fans: _____     Date/# of fans: _____     Date/# of fans: _____

Date/# of fans: _____     Date/# of fans: _____     Date/# of fans: _____

Date/# of fans: _____     Date/# of fans: _____     Date/# of fans: _____

# FACEBOOK POSTS TRACKING SHEET

<u>GOALS</u>. Write your goals in pencil so that you can change them over time.

Number of total posts/week (no less than 5 recommended): \_\_\_\_\_
Number of videos/week: \_\_\_
Number of articles/week: \_\_\_
Number of photos/week: \_\_
Number of polls/questions/week: \_\_\_
Number of announcements/week: \_\_\_

<u>TRACKING</u>. *Photocopy this sheet so that you can track over a long period of time.*

Week of: _____ # of total posts (no less than 5 recommended): \_\_\_\_\_
# of videos: _____          # of articles: \_\_\_\_\_          # of photos: \_\_\_\_\_
# of polls/questions: \_\_\_\_\_          # of announcements: \_\_\_\_\_

Week of: _____ # of total posts (no less than 5 recommended): \_\_\_\_\_
# of videos: _____          # of articles: \_\_\_\_\_          # of photos: \_\_\_\_\_
# of polls/questions: \_\_\_\_\_          # of announcements: \_\_\_\_\_

Week of: _____ # of total posts (no less than 5 recommended): \_\_\_\_\_
# of videos: _____          # of articles: \_\_\_\_\_          # of photos: \_\_\_\_\_
# of polls/questions: \_\_\_\_\_          # of announcements: \_\_\_\_\_

Week of: _____ # of total posts (no less than 5 recommended): \_\_\_\_\_
# of videos: _____          # of articles: \_\_\_\_\_          # of photos: \_\_\_\_\_
# of polls/questions: \_\_\_\_\_          # of announcements: \_\_\_\_\_

Week of: _____ # of total posts (no less than 5 recommended): \_\_\_\_\_
# of videos: _____          # of articles: \_\_\_\_\_          # of photos: \_\_\_\_\_
# of polls/questions: \_\_\_\_\_          # of announcements: \_\_\_\_\_

# YOUTUBE TRACKING SHEET

Date: _____          # of uploaded videos: _____
# of subscribers: _____   # of channel views: _____   # of upload views: _____
Name of most popular video: _____/# of views: _____


Date: _____          # of uploaded videos: _____
# of subscribers: _____   # of channel views: _____   # of upload views: _____
Name of most popular video: _____/# of views: _____


Date: _____          # of uploaded videos: _____
# of subscribers: _____   # of channel views: _____   # of upload views: _____
Name of most popular video: _____/# of views: _____


Date: _____          # of uploaded videos: _____
# of subscribers: _____   # of channel views: _____   # of upload views: _____
Name of most popular video: _____/# of views: _____


Date: _____          # of uploaded videos: _____
# of subscribers: _____   # of channel views: _____   # of upload views: _____
Name of most popular video: _____/# of views: _____


Date: _____          # of uploaded videos: _____
# of subscribers: _____   # of channel views: _____   # of upload views: _____
Name of most popular video: _____/# of views: _____


Date: _____          # of uploaded videos: _____
# of subscribers: _____   # of channel views: _____   # of upload views: _____
Name of most popular video: _____/# of views: _____


Date: _____          # of uploaded videos: _____
# of subscribers: _____   # of channel views: _____   # of upload views: _____
Name of most popular video: _____/# of views: _____

# TWITTER TRACKING SHEET

Date: _____    # of followers: _____    # you are following: _____
# of tweets/week: _____ # of "#"s/week: _____    # of "@" mentions/week: ____

Date: _____    # of followers: _____    # you are following: _____
# of tweets/week: _____ # of "#"s/week: _____    # of "@" mentions/week: ____

Date: _____    # of followers: _____    # you are following: _____
# of tweets/week: _____ # of "#"s/week: _____    # of "@" mentions/week: ____

Date: _____    # of followers: _____    # you are following: _____
# of tweets/week: _____ # of "#"s/week: _____    # of "@" mentions/week: ____

Date: _____    # of followers: _____    # you are following: _____
# of tweets/week: _____ # of "#"s/week: _____    # of "@" mentions/week: ____

Date: _____    # of followers: _____    # you are following: _____
# of tweets/week: _____ # of "#"s/week: _____    # of "@" mentions/week: ____

Date: _____    # of followers: _____    # you are following: _____
# of tweets/week: _____ # of "#"s/week: _____    # of "@" mentions/week: ____

Date: _____    # of followers: _____    # you are following: _____
# of tweets/week: _____ # of "#"s/week: _____    # of "@" mentions/week: ____

Date: _____    # of followers: _____    # you are following: _____
# of tweets/week: _____ # of "#"s/week: _____    # of "@" mentions/week: ____

Date: _____    # of followers: _____    # you are following: _____
# of tweets/week: _____ # of "#"s/week: _____    # of "@" mentions/week: ____

Date: _____    # of followers: _____    # you are following: _____
# of tweets/week: _____ # of "#"s/week: _____    # of "@" mentions/week: ____

# LINKEDIN TRACKING SHEET

Date: _____    % profile filled out: ____    # of connections: ____ # of groups: ___
# of recommendations: _____    # of recommendations you have written: _____

Date: _____    % profile filled out: ____    # of connections: ____ # of groups: ___
# of recommendations: _____    # of recommendations you have written: _____

Date: _____    % profile filled out: ____    # of connections: ____ # of groups: ___
# of recommendations: _____    # of recommendations you have written: _____

Date: _____    % profile filled out: ____    # of connections: ____ # of groups: ___
# of recommendations: _____    # of recommendations you have written: _____

Date: _____    % profile filled out: ____    # of connections: ____ # of groups: ___
# of recommendations: _____    # of recommendations you have written: _____

Date: _____    % profile filled out: ____    # of connections: ____ # of groups: ___
# of recommendations: _____    # of recommendations you have written: _____

Date: _____    % profile filled out: ____    # of connections: ____ # of groups: ___
# of recommendations: _____    # of recommendations you have written: _____

Date: _____    % profile filled out: ____    # of connections: ____ # of groups: ___
# of recommendations: _____    # of recommendations you have written: _____

Date: _____    % profile filled out: ____    # of connections: ____ # of groups: ___
# of recommendations: _____    # of recommendations you have written: _____

Date: _____    % profile filled out: ____    # of connections: ____ # of groups: ___
# of recommendations: _____    # of recommendations you have written: _____

# EVENT PROMOTION TRACKING SHEET
## (MASTER COPY)

*Make multiple copies of this sheet for future events.*

Name of event: _____

Date of event: _____

Check list for event promotion:
___ Facebook
___ Meetup
___ Eventbrite
___ Plancast
___ FindGravy.com
___ Evite or Mailchimp (to create invitations to send your email list)
___ Hootsuite
___ Twitter
___ LinkedIn
___ Website
___ Blog
___ YouTube (trailers, previews, promo videos)
___ YouTube (footage of the event)
___ Google+ events

Number of people in attendance: _____

Notes:

# NOTES

# APPENDIX D: RESOURCES

Here is a short list of resources for people and companies that you might outsource to help you with your social media and online marketing adventures.

## BASIC STRATEGY AND IMPLEMENTATION:

Coach Angela www.askcoachangela.net. Angela Schnauibelt is the author of this Playbook, and a fun marketing coach. Find an expanding list of resources on this website, adding to this list. Call (720) 722-3886 for a quick phone consultation.

Joyce Feustel http://boomerssocialmediatutor.com/. Joyce Feustel is a social media tutor for baby boomers and other business owners who want help setting up social media accounts. Joyce also teaches you how to use social media more effectively both for personal and business use.

## ADVANCED STRATEGY AND IMPLEMENTATION:

Joel Comm http://joelcomm.com/. Joel Comm, Twitter guru, is an accomplished speaker, prolific social media author, and all-around talented man: entrepreneur, consultant, and podcast host of the Joel Comm show. See his website for more books on social media, or hire him for a speaking engagement.

Bruce Barr http://www.unit304.com/index.html. Bruce Barr is a videographer who specializes in videos for your LinkedIn profile. He understands that even professional videos can get personal, and has a passion for production to accompany his experience.

Find more resources on www.askcoachangela.net.

# NOTES

# APPENDIX E: GLOSSARY

**Algorithm** – This is a formula that Google and other search engines use to determine which websites and which articles are most "useful" and "relevant" to the Internet user who is searching. Facebook also has algorithms to determine how to prioritize what shows up in the news feed on your timeline in accordance with how active you and your friends are with each other.

**Backlinks** – These are links on other websites that drive traffic to your website from other websites. Backlinks can be achieved any number of ways: website links in online directories; organic hyperlinks in articles; fans promoting your content to their friends; social bookmarking sites such as Reddit, StumbleUpon, Squidoo, Digg, etc.

**Blog** – Blog is short for "web log" and refers to more than a simple online journal. Blogs contain a content stream of timely and consistent submissions of articles, videos, comments, events, photos and more. Blog as a noun refers to the website that hosts the content, and "to blog" as a verb means the act of posting content on the website.

**Bounce Rate** – Reference to how fast a webpage visitor leaves. When visitors leave the page, it means that they immediately determine that they are either not interested or that they are looking for something else. High bounce rates indicate that the page is not maximized or that the keywords used to drive the traffic to the site are inappropriate.

**Browser** – The program on your computer with which you view websites on the Internet. You browse the Internet on a browser. Firefox and Chrome are examples of browsers.

**Campaign** – Organized effort towards a specific goal. Types of online marketing campaigns might include: Platform campaigns such as a YouTube campaign or Facebook campaign designed to ramp up fans and increase frequency of posting content; brand awareness campaigns; testimonial campaigns of video, photos, text containing stories and quotes, etc.

**Chrome**- This is an application (program) that you use to browse the Internet (hence the name browser). It is considered to be safer than Internet Explorer or AOL.

**Comment** – Posting a response, commentary, note of encouragement, etc. as a reaction to a blog post, article, another person's comment, or video. Comments can get very heated and lively on some news outlets and some high profile blogs.

**Connections** – This is the LinkedIn version of Facebook "friends" or YouTube "subscribers," or Twitter "followers." Connections refers to the people who are in your professional network that you have either done business with, done business for, or would like to connect and network with and hopefully do business with. Connections also refer to people who you have common interests with, thought leaders you may connect with in your industry, and people who are connections of connections that you might want to meet.

**Content** – Information and concise messages. Examples of content: articles, blogs, videos, comments, Facebook posts, tweets, photos.

**Conversion rate** – Refers to how many people are buying your service or acting on an opt-in, or clicking on your ad compared to total traffic.

**Craigslist** – Website where you can list your products and services for free. This is the online equivalent to classified advertising. Listings stay posted for two weeks then need reposting. Types of listings on Craigslist include services, goods, jobs, housing, ride-share.

**CTR** – Acronym for "Click Through Rate." The rate at which the number of clicks are performed on a set number of emails, tweets, etc. How many did you send out versus how many clicked on them?

**Demographics** – Your ideal customers are your demographics. For success with online marketing, it's critical to narrowly define your demographics so that you can target them with laser-like precision. This is called market segmentation for the purposes of appealing to prospects more effectively. Types of demographic categories might include: age, income, gender, geographical location, interests, buying habits, motives, etc.

**Directories** – Online directories are listings of businesses. Many are organized around geographical location; some are organized around broad themes such as health; yet others can be quite specific, such as yoga studios and teachers. Most directories are free to list your business, but ask for money if you want to be "featured" or "highlighted" for greater visibility.

**Domain** – As distinguished from your website host, the domain is who you pay to register the name of your website – your url, or address. (Some companies offer both)

**eBook** – "E" stands for electronic. Hence, an eBook is an electronic book. Some eBooks are only available in PDF form, some allow you to print the book at your own expense, yet others offer a print-on-demand feature where you can choose if you want to read the book online or read the printed version.

**Eventbrite** – Event listing website that enables attendees to RSVP and to print tickets. Eventbrite is free to list your event. If you charge for the event, the website takes a fee per ticket for processing it for you via PayPal.

**Facebook** – A social website with profiles where you build a profile and electronically befriend others (by simply accepting their friend requests). Facebook is the largest social media website in the world with over 1 billion users.

**Fans** – Name of a Facebook user who clicks "like" on your Business Fan Page. Facebook "fans" are equivalent to LinkedIn's "connections," Twitter's "followers," and YouTube's "subscribers."

**Firefox** – This is an application (program) that you use to browse the Internet (hence the name browser). Firefox is preferred by many as a safer and more private way to access the Internet than Internet Explorer or AOL.

**Followers** – Users on Twitter "follow" each other. This is a way of subscribing to people's public text messages (called "tweets") on the Twitter website. People can follow celebrities, companies, non-profit organizations, and other people – anyone or any company that has a Twitter account and posts messages. Twitter can be accessed via a cell phone or via a computer on the Internet. Followers are similar to Facebook "fans" and YouTube "subscribers."

**Forums** – Different than online chat rooms where the chat is live and in real-time, forums are websites that host discussions in the format of "discussion threads." Often, forums are organized around interests (e.g. gaming, lifestyle, health, technical specialties) and moderators and active participants offer expert advice and share knowledge. Forums can be used as bulletin boards, but usually are more dynamic in the discussions than static, offline bulletin boards.

**FourSquare** – A check-in site accessed by mobile phone users to announce their whereabouts to their friends, post reviews, and show loyalty to their favorite businesses. You can take advantage of this social application to list your business for free as well as offer a promotion if you choose. It's free for businesses to offer promotions and deals on FourSquare and is one way of cleverly encouraging and rewarding customer loyalty.

**Friends** – This is the Facebook version of LinkedIn "connections." Whereas fans are people who click "like" on your business Facebook fan page, "friends" are those who accept your friend request on your personal Facebook page.

**Google+** – This is a rich social network that, like Facebook, allows you to have a personal profile and a business profile to boost your branding campaign. Google+ gives you more traction in terms of SEO (search engine optimization), biases search results based on what websites your circle of friends (people in your Google+ network) have recommended, indexes content faster than other non-Google social networks, and offers users the ability to hangout and chat in web conferences.

**Graphics** – Online users are visual. Breaking up your text with interesting and professional graphics is very important in order to keep the visitor to your site engaged and interested. Videos are also important for this reason.

**Hashtag** – This is the pound sign (#) used on the social network Twitter as a way to mark a keyword or key phrase. For examples: "#asthma affects millions" – asthma is the keyword. Or, "alternative #asthmatreatements in this interesting article…" – asthma treatments is the key phrase. One advanced way to utilize the hashtag is to use it as a way to make a group of messages searchable (consult your professional Online Marketing Coach or Social Media Marketing Coach for more information).

**HootSuite** – A tool to manage your social media messages and leverage your time. This is especially useful when you have a team of social media helpers where you want some of the messages to get approval before being sent out, where you want to streamline campaigns, branding, and make sure that your messages are consistent. This social media management system is limited to Facebook, LinkedIn, Twitter, and Google+ pages.

**Host** – The website host, to be distinguished from the domain, is who offers you space on their server so that you can put content on your website. If you are putting up a lot of videos right on your website and not storing that huge amount of data on YouTube, then you may pay more money for the extra storage needs.

**Inbound Marketing** – Also called "permission-based" marketing, this is a form of pull (instead of push) marketing where customers come to you. Common inbound marketing tactics involve opt-ins for garnering email lists, free offers, SEO, micro-blogging, social media, sophisticated analytics, etc.

**Instagram** – Primarily a photo and video-sharing network, teenagers are migrating to this platform because of the ability to apply digital filters to their pictures and videos. From Instagram, you can then share your media to other social networking services such as Facebook and Twitter.

**Instant Messaging (IM)** – This is a form of real-time chat that is either text messages, or typing in a chat window. IM usually refers to a one-on-one dialog as opposed to real-time chatting in a chat room full of other people. Yahoo Messenger is one type of IM platform where someone might say, "ym me," meaning yahoo messenger me (send me a message via Yahoo Messenger so we can chat via that method). See "Ping" in this glossary, as well, for another way to say "send me a private chat message."

**Keywords** – These are words that are important in your content (article, tweet, comment, etc.). Keywords are what people use to search for something online and are therefore highly prized and critical in SEO (Search Engine Optimization) strategies. Keywords should be researched, as they can sometimes be counter-intuitive. For example: a chiropractor might use keywords of "back pain," "neck injuries," or "alternative asthma treatments" or "childhood ear infections" depending on what his demographics are.

**Like** – There is a button on Facebook where users can click "like" to indicate approval of the picture, video, comment, post, article, etc. Users can comment or share or like – or do all three. Like is a short, easy way to indicate approval without having to come up with a clever comment.

**Link Building** – This term is similar to backlinks, where website owners build up the number of links that drive traffic to their website. This is an important aspect of search engine optimization, as an increased number of backlinks remarkably improve the website's ranking in search results. Having a blog separate from your website is one primitive example of implementing link building.

**LinkedIn** – A social networking site that is oriented more for job seekers, professional networking, and business to business. LinkedIn is ranked #12 as most viewed website in the world according to Alexa.com. Having your profile filled out on LinkedIn is good business practice so as to increase your visibility online.

**Opt-ins** – This is the pop-up box or fill-in-your-email part of the page that makes you an offer for something free. You only get the freebie by opting-in to giving your email to them. This is a way to garner a valid email list of people interested in what you have to offer.

**Outsource** – To pay someone else to do an activity for you, usually used in terms of professional services. This differs from in-house marketing activities that you perform yourself.

**Pay Per Click Campaigns** – Also known as PPC campaigns. Just as it sounds, you decide how much you are willing to pay per click for each external click coming to your website from this type of advertising. This is a great way to control costs, as you only pay for advertising activity that is acted upon.

**Ping** – A verb that means you are being sent a message online in a chat application such as Yahoo Messenger. Instant messaging, or "IM" is synonymous to ping. Example: "ping me" means "message me," or "send me a private message."

**Pinterest** – A social bookmarking site for pictures and videos where users can organize the visuals onto virtual "bulletin boards" where they "pin" the content and also make comments. Pinterest can be used to promote contests that get your audience engaged and participating in your brand.

**Platforms** – When used in an online context, it refers to a vehicle with which to get your message out. You post content on platforms. Examples of platforms include Facebook, website, YouTube, etc.

**PPC** – Pay per Click campaign (see Pay per Click Campaign entry in this glossary).

**Professional Branding** – A brand is *your* unique identity as a company. A brand can include a logo design, a slogan or motto, your company or brand name, and even an "attitude" of your company or product. Red Bull, Nike, and Coca Cola are all great examples of successful corporate branding.

**Retweet** – Reposting someone else's interesting tweet that you get in your feed. It is a way to "forward" a tweet along to your followers. If you hover your mouse above the tweet that you are interested in, then the option to retweet appears. If you see "please rt" at the end of a tweet that means "please retweet." RT at the beginning of the message means that it is a retweet.

**Search Engine Optimization (SEO)** – This is a means of optimizing your content so that it can be found more easily by people searching on the Internet. SEO includes keywords, backlinking, cross-promoting, social bookmarking and other strategies that improve search engine rankings. Successful SEO implementation results in increased traffic *to* your website.

**Share** – When a user wants to share content with their friends and followers, social media platforms enable you to do this by clicking "share." Whereas a "like" is a passive approval of content, clicking "share" on Facebook, LinkedIn, YouTube, or Google+ posts the content to your news feed or timeline. This is similar to a "retweet," where a user is sharing a tweet.

**Shopping Cart** – Programming for your website that enables you to sell products online. Some shopping carts are templates that you can plug your products into and begin to sell right away, others are professionally built just for your unique situation. In most cases, you will need to invest in a shopping cart – free ones take a cut of your profits, so they aren't free, actually.

**Social Bookmarking** – This is a class of websites that have the possibility of helping your content go viral. Examples include: Delicious, Digg, Reddit, Facebook, StumbleUpon. Users of these websites share your content by either rating it with a thumbs up or thumbs down, or simply "share" the content to their friends. Social bookmark sites are usually included in SEO strategies.

**Social Media** – are online platforms that enable users to interact with each other by forming online communities, connecting to others with similar interests, keeping in contact with friends regardless of geographic location, and dialoging with others any time of the day or night. Examples are Facebook and Twitter.

**Social Media Monitoring** – is a way of listening and a way of monitoring what people are saying. This is a way of looking at statistics and analytics to understand trends, efficiency of ad campaigns, and refining demographics.

**StumbleUpon** – is a social bookmarking site that enables users to "bookmark" content for others to see and for others to stumble upon. Some call this an "intelligent browsing tool," yet others call it random promotion of content. It's actually both.

**Social Networking** – Networking through social media sites online. Often used interchangeably with social media. Social networking is the action of networking, whereas social media is the collection of platforms that enables you to network.

**Subscribers** – When used in the context of YouTube, it is similar to Facebook "fans" or "friends," or Twitter "followers." YouTube users can subscribe to your channel so that whenever you upload a video, they are notified. It's free to subscribe.

**Tools** – When used in the context of online tools, it refers to programming utilities, tactics, and anything that can make your activities on your online platforms more effective. A.video editing software would be an excellent tool, for example, for your videos achieve a higher conversion rate on YouTube. SEO is another example of a tool that is used to increase traffic to your website.

**Traffic** – When used in the context of online traffic, it refers to how many people are looking at your website. Similar to in-store traffic, some will buy but others are just browsing. This term ties in with the term "conversion rate."

**Twitter** – This is a social networking platform that allows users to text each other, and mass text messages to all of their followers. Texts are limited to 140 characters and therefore sometimes referred to as "micro-blogging" (a mini-blog, or a mini-blog post).

**URL** – This is the uniform resource locator, which just means the website address. Just as we have post office boxes and street addresses, this is the complete address where the website can be found. This is different than the domain name because the URL is the complete address, whereas the domain name is what is in between the www and the com.

**Video Blog or Vlog** – Different than a video or random video content on your YouTube channel, a vlog refers to a blog with a theme that contains video updates instead of article updates. A vlog can be hosted on your YouTube channel, on your website, or on a separate website that feeds into your website.

**Viral** – Content that is shared with a lot of people very quickly. For some people, an article that is viewed by several hundred people on a blog that usually gets less than 20 views is considered viral. For others, tens of thousands in just a few days is a viral success.

**Viral Marketing** – A guerilla marketing technique that promotes content to thought leaders and experts with high profile social media accounts with large numbers of followers, fans, subscribers, etc. The hope is that the content gets noticed, appreciated, and shared with others and goes "viral."

**Web Analytics** – A way to tangibly measure and analyze data such as number of people visiting the webpage (traffic), demographics of the traffic, origin of the traffic, conversion rates, keyword efficiency and more.

**Webinar** – Usually a live seminar or conference that contains voice and sometimes video (either PowerPoint slides, live webcam, or other video) and enables attendees to ask questions and participate. Webinars can take the form of live meetings, presentations, training, and classes.

**Yelp** – This is a website that allows users to post reviews of businesses. Reviews contain a five star rating system, space to write opinions and suggestions, and rave about or complain. Yelp allows business owners the opportunity to respond to reviews publicly. Yelp and other review sites are a great way to increase your online presence by filling out the profile completely with keywords, descriptions, photos and sometimes videos.

**YouTube** – The third most-viewed website in the world according to Alexa.com, YouTube hosts videos that are uploaded by users for free. Google, Inc. now owns YouTube. Business owners can create a "channel" just like anybody else, and there is no prohibition for blatantly promoting your product or service. It's best to launch a coordinated marketing campaign, though, as social media etiquette still applies. See your Social Media Coach or Online Marketing Coach for more information.

# NOTES

# APPENDIX F: COACH ANGELA'S MARKETING MANTRAS

- "Begin with the end in mind."

- "Slow and steady wins the race."

- "Take the long view."

- "Stand in your truth," or "Stay in your truth."

- "Be authentic, be yourself."

- "There are no shortcuts to marketing."

- "Selling is easy, salespeople make it hard."

- "Reality is where you put your attention."

- "Stay the course."

- "Start with the big picture, then create a strategy. Only then can you go forth and implement."

- "Eat an elephant one bite at a time."

- "A journey of a thousand miles begins with one step."

- "Play big or go home."

- "Practice judgment-free awareness."

www.ingramcontent.com/pod-product-compliance
Lightning Source LLC
Chambersburg PA
CBHW080418270326

41929CB00018B/3075